AIR FORCE
LIVES

FAMILY HISTORY FROM PEN & SWORD

How Our Ancestors Lived

AIR FORCE LIVES

A Guide for Family Historians

Phil Tomaselli

Pen & Sword
FAMILY HISTORY

First published in Great Britain in 2013 by
PEN & SWORD FAMILY HISTORY
an imprint of
Pen & Sword Books Ltd
47 Church Street
Barnsley
South Yorkshire
S70 2AS

ISBN 978 1 84884 743 9

A CIP catalogue record for this book is
available from the British Library.

Typeset in Palatino and Optima by
Phoenix Typesetting, Auldgirth, Dumfriesshire

Printed and bound in England by
CPI Group (UK) Ltd, Croydon, CR0 4YY

Pen & Sword Books Ltd incorporates the Imprints of Pen & Sword Aviation, Pen &
Sword Family History, Pen & Sword Maritime, Pen & Sword Military, Pen &
Sword Discovery, Wharncliffe Local History, Wharncliffe True Crime,
Wharncliffe Transport, Pen & Sword Select, Pen & Sword Military Classics, Leo
Cooper, The Praetorian Press, Remember When, Seaforth Publishing and
Frontline Publishing

For a complete list of Pen & Sword *titles please contact*
PEN & SWORD BOOKS LIMITED
47 Church Street, Barnsley, South Yorkshire, S70 2AS, England
E-mail: enquiries@pen-and-sword.co.uk
Website: www.pen-and-sword.co.uk

CONTENTS

ACKNOWLEDGEMENTS

As ever, I owe a great deal of thanks to a number of individuals who have helped me with the researching of this book. Andrew Salmond Smith introduced me to the story of his grandfather, David Prosser Hepburn, and the mystery of his Military Medal, and kindly allowed me to reproduce his photograph; Will Hepburn was very helpful and gave me additional information about his father's life, as did his grandson, David Hepburn; Margaret Gregory kindly allowed me to use the research that I did for her into her uncle, Vic Reid; Martyn Ford-Jones, Official Historian of 15 Squadron, generously permitted me access to his own researches and provided the photographs; the late Martin Kender introduced me to Janet Boddy (formerly Pegden) and Peter Hart of the Imperial War Museum gave me access to the interview he'd done with her; Rosemary Horrell showed me the papers of her late stepfather, Group Captain Bone, many years ago and sparked my long interest into both his fascinating career and aviation generally; Roy Hemington at the Commonwealth War Graves Commission provided information from its records; veteran medal researcher Paul Baillie kindly found the medal citation for Wilfred Beale and Bill Cleland's crew in the AIR 2 records; the late Guy Blampied provided me with transcripts of his Russia diaries, photographs of the campaign and gave me much information in the course of several telephone calls to him at his home on Guernsey. Dr John Salt helpfully trawled records in Horsham for information on the ME 109 shot down by Guy Marsland. Ian Piper kindly provided a photograph of Tom Beale. Barbara Chambers showed me her mother's and father's service records and photographs and introduced me to her brother, Colin, who, with the benefit of long RAF service himself, was able to pass on to me many of the stories his father had told him. Helen Cleland introduced me to her husband, Bill, who sadly passed away during the writing of this book and to his bomb-aimer and lifetime friend, Jack Watson, who loaned me his log book and memoir (from which I've quoted extensively). The staff at The National Archives have been, as ever, friendly, professional and knowledgeable.

My wife Francine has had to live with my interest in some of the people featured in the book for well over twenty years and has accompanied me on visits to archives, museums, obscure airfields and monuments, the French coast and the Somme battlefields carrying out research without a word of complaint. I could not have done it without her and am pleased to be able to dedicate this work to her.

ABBREVIATIONS AND WEBSITES

List of Abbreviations

AAF	Auxiliary Air Force
FAA	Fleet Air Arm
IWM	Imperial War Museum
ORB	Operational Record Book
OTC	Officers' Training Corps
RAF	Royal Air Force
RFC	Royal Flying Corps
RNAS	Royal Naval Air Service
TNA	The National Archives
WAAF	Women's Auxiliary Air Force

Useful Websites

Discovery facility, TNA	http://discovery.nationalarchives.gov.uk/SearchUI/
Flight magazine	http://www.flightglobal.com
Imperial War Museum	http://www.iwm.org.uk
London Gazette	http://www.london-gazette.co.uk
Royal Air Force	http://www.raf.mod.uk
The National Archives	http://www.nationalarchives.gov.uk

INTRODUCTION

When I was first asked to write this book, I wasn't, initially, sure I wanted to do it. I'd spent many years researching RAF records generally for my book *Tracing your Air Force Ancestors* (Pen and Sword, 2007) and wasn't sure there was much I could add. Once I thought about it a bit more, however, I realised that some of the people I'd mentioned in that book deserved a more in-depth treatment if their stories were to be adequately told, and I had several other people I'd started researching whose Air Force lives deserved more work. The range of people represented covers, I hope, many of the aspects of the air forces from before the First World War through to the 1970s, giving interesting examples of the types of people who served and the jobs that they did. By using a wide range of sources I hope also to show other researchers the kind of stories that can be built up and I would urge anyone who is researching an Air Force ancestor to write them up for the benefit of others as well. If nothing else, I trust the stories of the men and women here are interesting and informative and as much a pleasure to read as they have been to research and write.

A BRIEF HISTORY OF
THE AIR FORCES
FEATURED IN THIS BOOK

Although the first proper aeroplane was flown in December 1903 by the American Wright brothers, it was only after a visit by Wilbur Wright to France in 1908 to demonstrate the aircraft that inspired imitators really began to build other machines. In 1908 an American named Samuel Cody, working for the British Army, flew an aeroplane of his own design at Farnborough. His experiments continued until his death in an air crash in 1913 but by that time his models were being superseded by machines designed and built abroad. Flying schools sprang up across the country and a generation of young men, many of them army and navy officers, learnt to fly. Bleriot's cross-Channel flight in 1909 sparked worries that the Channel was no longer a defence Britain could depend upon and newspapers and the public demanded a military response. On 1 April 1911 the Air Battalion of the Royal Engineers was formed with an airship company based at Farnborough and an aeroplane company at Larkhill.

The Air Battalion existed for only a year because in 1912 the Royal Flying Corps (RFC) was formed, a joint venture between the army and Royal Navy, with a Military and a Naval Wing. The world's first military flying school, the Central Flying School, was established at Upavon on Salisbury Plain, with a joint navy and army staff. A scheme was created whereby army and navy officers could learn to fly at their own expense and, on qualifying, would receive £75 to cover the costs. Reginald Bone, the naval officer we meet in Chapter 1, qualified as a pilot under this scheme after transferring from the Submarine Service to the Naval Wing of the RFC. The arrangement worked well for a while, but in 1914 the RN created the Royal Naval Air Service (RNAS) as a separate service and, for most of the First World War, the two services remained separate, though they did cooperate with each other.

On the outbreak of the First World War the RFC (now purely for the army) went to France with 4 squadrons, 63 aircraft and approximately 900 men. A rapid training programme was established to produce pilots, observers and ground crew so there were 12 squadrons by September 1915 and 27 squadrons, with over 600 aircraft, by the start of the Battle of the Somme in July 1916. David Hepburn served with two RFC squadrons during the Somme engagement and won his Military Medal there.

Aircraft gradually became specialised as fighter, bomber or reconnaissance models, and the squadrons specialised accordingly. Developments in engines, cameras, clothing and weaponry meant that the aircraft of 1918 were technologically much more advanced than the ones originally sent to France in 1914. As well as their squadrons in France, the RFC sent men and aircraft to the Middle East, Italy and the Balkans, with special missions also being deployed to Russia to train their Flying Corps, and to Canada for recruitment and training.

There was a constant race between the opposing flying services with periods when one or the other was in the ascendancy. At times, a new pilot's life expectancy on being sent to the Western Front could be measured in days. New training techniques (see Chapter 4 featuring Wilfred 'Tom' Beale) gradually improved the situation.

With the departure of the entire fighting strength of the RFC to France in August, defence of Britain passed, by agreement, to the RNAS. Fortunately for the young RNAS pilots in their poorly armed machines, the expected Zeppelin raids did not materialise until early 1915.

In October 1914 an RNAS squadron was sent to Dunkirk to support the Royal Naval division that was operating in Belgium and this grew into a large RNAS presence of several squadrons that became 5 Group RNAS.

During 1915 RNAS aircraft flew and fought at Gallipoli, on the Turkish coast, and patrolled the British coast for German submarines and raiding aircraft. With the start of the Zeppelin attacks they also mounted night patrols but were generally unable to intercept the high-flying airships.

During 1916, as well as their air-defence responsibilities (taken back by the RFC later in the year), the RNAS began strategic bombing raids from France against German steelworks in the Rhineland. They had some success but the terrible casualties suffered by the RFC during the later stages of the Somme fighting meant that they were diverted for service under the army. Several RNAS squadrons flew with the RFC in a fighter role and the RNAS produced their own crop of fighter aces.

By 1918 RNAS units were serving in the Middle East, in the Aegean, in France and in Italy. They had aircraft operating from a number of ships, including seaplane carriers and planes launched from platforms mounted on battleships and cruisers. The first aircraft carrier as we would recognise it today was close to completion.

Following two serious German daytime air raids on London in 1917, in which the attackers were virtually unmolested, an enquiry under Field Marshal Smuts recommended the amalgamation of the RFC and RNAS. On 1 April 1918 they formally amalgamated to become the Royal Air Force (RAF).

On 11 November 1918 the RAF comprised 188 squadrons, 22,000 aircraft and nearly 300,000 officers and men. It was rapidly cut to just 33 squadrons. Hugh Trenchard, who had commanded the RFC in France for most of the war, was appointed to head it.

Trenchard was determined the fledgling service would survive and grow. He created a Technical School at Halton and an Officers School at Cranwell. All officers were expected to be able to fly and other ranks were carefully recruited via advertisements in technical journals. Everyone was expected to spend at least part of their service overseas.

Trenchard, pointing to a cheap and successful RAF campaign in Somaliland against 'native' forces, suggested the RAF be given a free hand in Iraq, which was in a state of almost perpetual low-level revolt. In 1922 command in Iraq was given to an RAF officer with 8 squadrons of aircraft, supported by a few British and Indian troops, local levies and armoured cars. When rebellion occurred, the RAF (after dropping warnings) would bomb hostile towns and villages and strafe rebel troops. Though there was some debate at home about the ethics of attacking defenceless villages, the saving in British lives and money was generally recognised.

The other main posting for the RAF between the wars was India.

At any one time there were usually eight or nine RAF squadrons serving in India and, as in Iraq, they played their role in keeping the peace or in assisting the army in a series of small wars. Ernest 'Jerry' Chambers (see Chapter 6) served in the final campaigns before the Second World War.

During the 1920s and 1930s the RAF played an important part in the development of aviation. Long-distance flights were made to Cape Town and the Far East. The RAF in Iraq pioneered Air Mail by carrying mail from Cairo to Baghdad. The Auxiliary Air Force (AAF) was formed in 1924 to provide a reserve of trained pilots (see Chapter 4, Wilfred 'Tom' Beale served in an AAF unit in the 1930s).

During the 1930s the prospect of another European war loomed and a policy of expansion was begun in 1933. New stations were built to house an expanded service and in just 2 years another 2,200 pilots and 20,000 other ranks were recruited. New aircraft were commissioned to replace the RAF's ageing aeroplanes. Among the new planes were the Hawker Hurricane and Supermarine Spitfire and a new generation of heavy bombers, such as the Stirling and Halifax. On the outbreak of war the RAF had 157 squadrons with nearly 2,000 front-line aircraft, though only 270 were Hurricanes and 240 Spitfires. At the height of the war some 110,000 officers and 1,050,000 other ranks were serving in the RAF.

At home, there were three main fighting commands. Fighter Command was formed in July 1936 under Air Marshall Sir Hugh Dowding, and its main role was the air defence of Britain. Dowding built a superb organisation with fighter groups defending specific regions and sector control operation rooms controlling groups of fighters by voice radio. Close links with the Observer Corps and radar stations, Balloon Command and anti-aircraft defences created a sophisticated defence system. During the Battle of Britain it was the resilience and flexibility of Fighter Command's organisation and communications and the hard work and ability of the men and women at ground level who managed the aircraft and aerodromes and maintained the communications and kept 'The Few' in the air. Their contribution to the battle should not be overlooked. Guy Marsland (see Chapter 5) flew Hurricanes throughout the whole of 1940 and participated in the final stage of the Battle of Britain.

Bomber Command carried the war to Germany. The RAF's own website explains the reasons for the four-year campaign:

to disrupt industrial production of weapons, to wear down the German people's morale and to force the German Army and Air Force (the Luftwaffe) into having to defend against the bombing over a wide area. Repeated attacks on the German homeland also caused the diversion of industrial war production to defensive rather than offensive weapons and equipment. Forcing the Germans onto the defensive was a critical factor in the liberation of Europe and the defeat of Nazi Germany in 1945.

Both Vic Reid and Bill Cleland's Pathfinder crew (see Chapters 7 and 8) flew numerous dangerous missions with Bomber Command.

Coastal Command was responsible for land-based, long-range reconnaissance of the sea lanes, as well as for land-based bombers and torpedo bombers of the RAF flying in support of the RN. Their flying boats (originally mainly Short Sunderlands and later Catalinas) escorted convoys and made independent reconnaissance and anti-submarine patrols. As the Battle of the Atlantic raged Coastal Command used long-range bombers to carry the anti-submarine war into the very centre of the Atlantic. Their Beaufighters and other aircraft ranged far and wide attacking enemy shipping with cannon, rockets and torpedoes.

In addition to these main fighting commands, there were other support commands: Training Command and Maintenance Command (with obvious roles), Balloon Command, which ran the barrage balloons that defended cities and other targets, Ferry & Transport Command, which moved aircraft and equipment and troops by air, and a short-lived Army Cooperation Command, which controlled the RAF squadrons that worked closely with the army. Outside Britain there were individual commands covering different geographical areas. It was perfectly possible to serve in more than one command during a career – Guy Marsland, for example, served in Fighter Command but also in South East Asia Command, Training Command and Coastal Command (see Chapter 5).

After the war the RAF continued to have a worldwide role, now flying mainly jet aircraft. Guy Marsland served with an RAF Mission to Greece in the late 1940s and Jerry Chambers (see Chapter 6) served in Egypt, the Far East, Cyprus, Libya and Germany before he retired in 1972, just as major contractions to Britain's defence commitments abroad really began to bite.

The Fleet Air Arm

From 1918 to 1937 the aircraft carried by the RN's aircraft carriers were flown and controlled by the RAF; originally called 'Naval Air Contingents', in 1924 their title was changed to 'Fleet Air Arm' (FAA). In addition to the carriers, FAA officers and men manned the individual aircraft that were carried by bigger ships of the fleet. The RAF provided most of the pilots for the FAA, although navy officers were supposed to play a significant role, but their career structure did not encourage them to take the time to learn to fly and to serve in something that was not considered really a part of the RN.

In 1937, after nearly twenty years of debate, it was decided to return the FAA to the Admiralty and this took place with effect from May 1939. Naval officers were now encouraged to take an active part, though when war was declared in September 1939 the FAA had still not trained sufficient technical 'ground crew' and had to borrow from the RAF. The FAA went into the Second World War with six operational carriers though only one, the *Ark Royal* was a truly modern ship.

During the course of Second World War the FAA fought in every ocean, loaned pilots to the RAF during the Battle of Britain, helped to sink the German raider *Bismarck,* flew off tiny carriers to escort convoys in the Battle of the Atlantic and attacked the Italian Battle Fleet in its home port of Taranto, torpedoing three Italian battleships and crippling the fleet. In 1945, as the tide turned against Japan, FAA planes carried out their largest ever air raid against oil refineries at Palembang on Sumatra and other carriers and aircraft supported American operations against Okinawa and the Japanese mainland until Japan's surrender in August 1945.

At the end of Second World War the FAA had 52 operational carriers and 3,243 pilots and had earned its place as a permanent arm of the RN. When Janet Boddy (see Chapter 9) served with the FAA in the 1950s it was gradually moving into the jet age.

A General Note on Sources

Specific notes on sources of information for individuals are given in each chapter, but it's worth saying something generally. Researchers are blessed with a vast number of official and unofficial sources from which both general and specific information can be gleaned. An increasing amount of information is also available online, both in terms of some early service records and official squadron histories and a great many unofficial, but generally excellently researched, private websites on squadrons and air stations. Having said that, the air force has been sadly neglected by the two big genealogy websites, Ancestry and Findmypast, so you will have to do a lot of digging through original paperwork – which to my mind adds to the fun, but will involve travelling to The National Archives (TNA) at Kew.

For the First World War period and earlier, service records for RAF officers are in TNA's AIR 76 series which is available online via TNA's website at http://www.nationalarchives.gov.uk. Records for ordinary airmen are in AIR 79, which is not online but is (despite rumours to the contrary) pretty much comprehensive for men who served with the RAF before the early 1920s. The few surviving records for the Women's Royal Air Force in the First World War are available on TNA website. Service records from after the early 1920s will have to be applied for and the process is explained in the Chapter 5.

The main records covering RAF stations and squadrons (an individual was generally appointed to one or the other, especially early in their career) are available at TNA in AIR 28 series (stations) and Air 27 (squadrons). Most AIR 27 records have recently become available online at TNA's website. Other records that may have useful information are in AIR 1 series, which contains just about everything from the First World War for the RFC and RNAS; Air 25, which contains records of RAF groups and which provide a high level appreciation of what was going on; and AIR 29, which contains records of the multitudinous support units of the RAF from training schools, embarkation units, maintenance units and the RAF Regiment. Surviving combat records from the Second World War for all categories of RAF aircraft are in AIR 50 series and are available online via TNA's website.

The RAF Museum at Hendon has a splendid collection of donated material, as does the Imperial War Museum (IWM) and both also have extensive collections of photographs.

There are far too many excellent books on individuals, squadrons, battles, aircraft and stations to begin to make a comprehensive list. Your local library can probably obtain copies of the rarer ones via the excellent Inter Library Loans Service; don't be afraid to use these books, if only as a starting point for further original research.

The whole period covered in this book is one of mass-media coverage. Local and national newspapers have always known that aeroplanes make good copy and they should be consulted for stories with local connections. There are extensive collections of film on aviation – the IWM has many such films and their catalogue is worth checking via their website at http://www.iwm.org.uk/collections/search.

There are also hundreds of official and unofficial websites devoted to aviation matters. First and foremost is the RAF's own website at http://www.raf.mod.uk, which has numerous pages devoted to the service's history and units.

Chapter 1

EARLY FLYING EXPERIENCES IN THE ROYAL NAVAL AIR SERVICE – REGINALD BONE

eggie Bone first flew in 1912 and was still working in the aviation industry forty years later, a period spanning the earliest ramshackle Bleriot monoplanes, on which he learned to fly, and the jet engine, on which he worked in the 1950s. Though his career was long and fascinating, here we concentrate on his early experiences as a pilot, derived, in part, from his unpublished memoirs.

Reggie was born in Dorking in 1888, the son of an East India merchant. His older brother, Archie, was intended to take over the business (though he actually joined the Indian Army) so Reggie was educated privately, intending to join the RN. He passed the exams and in 1904 became a cadet on HMS *Britannia*. Forerunner of the modern Naval College, *Britannia* was an old wooden three-decker anchored at Dartmouth and aboard her he learned the basics of seamanship and leadership. Described as 'zealous, hard working, slow in study', he obtained First Class results in Seamanship and Torpedoes, Second Class in Gunnery and Third Class in Pilotage.

Qualifying as a midshipman, he served on the armoured cruisers *Donegal* and *Devonshire* and pre-Dreadnought battleships HMS *Russell* and HMS *Majestic*, then the destroyer *Foam* in the Mediterranean.

Reggie realised the Submarine Service offered opportunities for a keen, young officer to get early responsibility and promotion and, volunteering for it, was posted to *HMS Dolphin*, the Submarine School at Gosport. Having completed his basic training, he was appointed as second officer on submarine *C1* based at Sheerness.

1

Reggie Bone (in striped scarf) with the First Captain and crew of submarine C1, 1913. (Courtesy of Mrs Rosemary Horrell)

While serving in submarines, Reggie conceived the idea of learning to fly. Though initially reluctant to support aviation, the Admiralty had agreed to reimburse retrospectively the sum of £75 provided the candidate passed their Brevet (pilot's licence). This cannily saved them the expenses of pilots who didn't pass the test. Learning to fly was undoubtedly dangerous; aircraft were primitive, training techniques were basic and there was serious risk of fatal accident – of the first 100 pilots qualifying in Britain, 11 were subsequently killed in accidents.

Reggie became a pupil at the Eastbourne Aviation Company, a small south-coast school, established in December 1911 by Bernard Fowler, who'd taught himself to fly and become Chief Instructor. Though the school was only small (turning out just six qualified pupils in 1912), it had a good reputation. One of the instructors there was J J Hammond, a New Zealander who'd learned to fly at the Bristol Aviation Company School on Salisbury Plain and made the first serious flights in Australia, where on his first flight he flew across Sydney Harbour. The main workshop of the aerodrome was a converted corrugated iron church with offices, a pupils' changing room, a sitting room for pupils and a mechanics' mess room. In May 1913 they were equipped with three Bleriot monoplanes, a Bristol biplane and their own aircraft, the EAC monoplane, and were building three Henry Farman seaplanes ready for the summer season. *Flight* magazine described it as, 'A splendid aerodrome, plenty of machines, a first class instructor whose heart is in his work, every convenience, and jolly companions . . . I think learning to fly is indeed a pleasure at Eastbourne'. From Reggie's point of view, based as he was at

Sheerness, Eastbourne was probably more convenient than the larger schools at Hendon.

Initial training comprised learning to control the aircraft on the ground and Reggie's first few lessons were in steering the aeroplane, an old Bleriot monoplane. He was then expected to make some short 'hops' to get used to being a few feet off the ground.

Flight magazine, which reported on most aviation schools, recorded, on 22 June 1912,

> On Wednesday last week, Lieut Bone and Gassler were both out, the former putting in some good rolling practice and the latter excellent short flights. Thursday, Friday and Saturday were all too rough for outdoor work, but on Sunday the weather improved considerably towards the evening, when Lieut Bone was able to put in some more practice. He showed a marked improvement towards the end of the evening and was doing hops in great style.

On 29 June *Flight* recorded: 'On Saturday evening the weather conditions were perfect, and Lieuts Bone and Brown and Mr Gassler put in some good practice. Sunday evening saw them all out again, when Lieut Bone took his first flight, which nearly ended in disaster to the Anzani.' Reggie described the incident,

> At Eastbourne the equipment was the Bleriot monoplane which was difficult to keep straight while running on the ground. In consequence the pupils first process was what were termed straight rolls in an old aircraft which was no longer considered fit to fly. One evening I was doing my straight rolls on a 25 hp Anzani Bleriot when an unexpected gust lifted me 50 ft off the ground – pointing at the local gas works. I had had no instruction in the air and all I knew was what I had heard in conversation. I contrived to make a half circuit and made a faultless landing, at which the engine coughed and stopped.

Though Hammond ran from the clubhouse shouting and swearing and threatened never to have him at the school again, Reggie was able to placate him and continue his training.

On 7 July *Flight* reported,

On Wednesday last week the wind was too strong for practice, but Thursday morning was dead calm and the machines were out at 4 am . . . Lieut Bone made his first flight most successfully but landed outside the ground, fortunately doing no damage. In the evening . . . Lieut Bone made several short flights, but did not manage the machine quite as well as he did in the morning.

On Friday practice again commenced early . . . Lieut Bone made a short flight but found the wind rather trying. Mr Fowler then had the 50 hp Gnome-Bleriot out. By this time the wind had freshened considerably, and in trying to start with the wind on his beam, the machine side slipped and came down on one wing, smashing the whole of the landing chassis as well as the propeller and wing. Further practice was rendered impossible by the wind. In the evening . . . Lieut Bone landed rather heavily and put one of the Anzanis out of action. On Saturday . . . Lieut Bone was doing short straights. Sunday morning saw Lieuts Bone and Brown out again and Mr Gassler out again.

On 9 September *Flight* reported,

On Friday evening . . . Lieut Bone was doing straights on the 25 hp Anzani. Saturday turned out a beautiful day, and the pupils got in some useful practice. Lieut Bone tried the 28 hp for the first time, and after one or two runs was able to do straights in good style. [On Sunday] Mr Bone was doing straights on the 28 hp in excellent style.

On 12 October *Flight* reported:

On Saturday, Lieut Bone took on the 28 hp Anzani, flew on circuit, landing well. Next day [Lieutenant Murray] made several solos in the Bristol doing right and left turns with perfect confidence. Lieut Bone and Messrs Gassler and Foggin were hard at it in the 28 hp Anzani.

Tuesday Mr Foggin flew in the morning, and in the afternoon Mr Hammond flew over to Bexhill with Mr Bone, while Mr Fowler was out amusing spectators in the evening.

The onset of winter and naval commitments seem to have prevented Reggie from flying until August 1913, when he returned to Eastbourne to test for his Brevet (pilot's licence). On 16 August *Flight* recorded: 'On Thursday morning, Fowler had Lieut Bone RN and Mr Beavis up on the EAC biplane by turns. Lieut Bone then went up with Gassler, and Mr Fill was doing straights on the 35 hp Bleriot.' On 28 August:

> On Wednesday morning, Gassler had the EAC biplane out, taking up in turns, Messrs Blevis and Thornley and Lieut Bone.
> Friday, Fowler had Mr Thornley up twice, Lieut Bone up twice and Messrs Bevis and Hunt once . . . Gassler had the biplane out and took up Lieut Bone and Messrs Thornley, Bevis, Hunt and Wood. Lieut Bone then did a couple of circuits solo.
> Saturday morning . . . Lieut Bone accomplished his brevet in fine style, landing practically on the mark each time.

The basic test to secure one's Brevet involved a series of take-offs and landings followed by a figure of eight flight round a marked course, followed by a landing on a mark on the runway. Aerobatics were virtually unheard of and the exam only tested basic flying competency.

Reggie was awarded Royal Aero Club Aviator's Certificate 627, dated 16 August 1913. His appointment to the Central Flying School for a course of additional instruction commencing in September 1913 was announced by the Admiralty on 15 August. Reggie recalls in his memoirs,

> After I got my Brevet I applied to the Commodore (S) to transfer to the RNAS, which was strongly resisted. His case was that the Navy had expended money in training me for submarine work and that I must remain in submarines. My case was that when I volunteered for submarines in 1909 there was no flying to volunteer for. The dispute ended in my being taken to the 2nd Sea Lord's Office at the Admiralty, where I won my case that one could not retain a volunteer against his wish. I went to the Central Flying School at Upavon a fortnight later, in September 1913.

A report by the School Commandant details the instruction given to the pupils. Working in groups of seven, the officers spent three weeks in the workshops studying the mechanics of various Gnome, Renault and Anzani engines, the mounting and dismounting of engines, the construction of aeroplanes, the dismantling, repair and truing up of aircraft and the examination of aeroplanes for defects, along with their correction. A total of sixty-two lectures were attended, covering theory of flight, meteorology, internal combustion engines, aerial navigation and use of maps, care of aeroplanes, hints on flying, rules of the air and aerodrome and aerial reconnaissance. Other lectures concentrated on subjects of a purely military nature, such as observing artillery fire, troop formations and types of warships.

Officers flew an average of 23 hours 23 minutes over the period of the course and the average standard of efficiency obtained in handling the various types of machine was very high, the majority of officers being proficient in more than one type of machine. Most flying was carried out near to dawn or dusk, when wind conditions were considered most favourable. Many years later, the author had the pleasure of hearing from the son of Lieutenant Williamson, who recalled how, as a small boy, his mother had taken him to Upavon to see his father and other pilots waiting, at dawn, for the wind to drop so they could take off.

At the end of the course the officers sat practical exams in flying, map reading, use of the compass, engines and signalling on a

Short tractor (propeller at the front) seaplane approaching the beach at Great Yarmouth, with Reggie Bone at the controls. (Courtesy of Mrs Rosemary Horrell)

buzzer. Written exams were in theory of flight, internal combustion engines and strength of materials, formation of troops, aerial reconnaissance and meteorology. All but two officers passed (one, Major G C Merrick, having been killed in a flying accident). The Commandant noted on Reggie's service record, 'Very keen officer. VG knowledge of internal combustion engines. Good pilot.'

After a month at the RNAS station on the Isle of Grain training to fly seaplanes, Reggie was posted to the air station at Great Yarmouth, recently created and based on the beach south of the town. Seaplanes were slid down the beach into the sea for take-off and, on occasion, took townsfolk for short flights at the price of a shilling! In March 1914 Reggie, flying in a Maurice Farman Longhorn, came down about 40 miles from Yarmouth near the village of Saxmundham, tearing off his tail plane and elevators on a tree stump. A rating from the station, sent out to help, recorded a rescue mission that recalls a Keystone Kops movie and shows the flimsy and makeshift nature of early aeroplanes,

> Four of us were dispatched in a Crossley tender with lengths of spruce to effect repairs. Passing through Resingland village at top speed, we knocked down an old man carrying a cross-cut saw, veered round and demolished a blacksmith's shop, bending the front axle and rendering the tender useless. The old man was picked up, taken home, well soaked in brandy, and put to bed, while one of the party 'phoned for assistance. Mr Courtney arrived in a cloud of dust with his racing car, and ordered us to transfer the tools and material to his car. That meant five of us in a two-seater racer with a smooth body. We had two punctures before reaching Saxmundham – adding to Mr Courtney's amiability. Luckily the timber was broken off exactly the required length in the smithy crash, which eased tempers considerably, and with the help of a few tree branches, and of a nice farm wench who machined the fabric for us, we completed the job. Mr Bone took off in a ploughed field with about a 50 yard run and sailed between two trees with wingtips almost touching. After experiencing three more punctures, we arrived at Yarmouth, having changed our car again for a private conveyance. We always thought that Mr Bone had the laugh on us on that trip, but that take-off of his was worth going a long way to see.

Maurice Farman pusher (the propeller faced backwards) with a group of onlookers on the beach at Great Yarmouth. (Courtesy of Mrs Rosemary Horrell)

On 1 April 1914 Reggie was making take-offs and landings in a Sopwith seaplane No. 60 from the beach at the air station when disaster struck. The *Yarmouth Mercury* recorded,

YARMOUTH SEAPLANE WRECKED

One of the Yarmouth seaplanes was, on Wednesday afternoon, beached in a much damaged condition at Caister-On-Sea. During the afternoon Lieutenant Bone made two or three ascents in the vicinity of the Naval Air-craft Station. On the last occasion all went well until he was near the St Nicholas Lightship, when there was an ominous sound of something going wrong. The machine was then allowed to drift, the engine having been switched off and Lieutenant Bone was taken aboard the Flying Corps' motor launch. It was afterwards ascertained that one of the floats of the seaplane had been stove in.

Lieutenant Bone stated it was just an ordinary accident, which might occur at any moment, as seaplanes are only in their infancy, but in a couple of years, when they are perfected, it would probably not be known. A seaplane, he explained, has to rise against the wind, and when the engine is turned on to gain the requisite impetus to soar, the floats, which on this seaplane are of three-ply wood, have to encounter the blows of the waves, and in this instance the material yielded to the continual thumping to which it was exposed. It would have been possible to rise with a damaged float, but if the pilot had to descend with one in this condition it would become water-logged and capsize. He was not, he said, in any danger, and if the worst had happened, he would have swum to the shore. From the spot where the mishap occurred to the place where the machine was beached at Caister, he estimated was a distance of four miles. This was one of the risks incidental to seaplanes in their present state of development, in which they differ from aeroplanes and machines used for flying from land.

One steamer passed him while he was in the disabled machine before help reached him from the launch, and offered no assistance. This, however, may be due to the fact it was not realised on board that the seaplane was in difficulties, there being no contrivance for showing a signal of distress.

In May 1914 Reggie (mistakenly named as Beaumann by *Flight*) flew a Maurice Farman biplane to Norwich where the pioneer aviator Mr B C Hucks and his assistant Marcus Manton were demonstrating the new technique of looping the loop. Flying Bleriot monoplanes, the two men flew upside down, raced each other, looped the loop and performed other daring feats. Reggie himself drew some attention, and according to the *Eastern Daily Press*, 'The arrival just after three o'clock of a biplane from Yarmouth Naval Aviation Station caused a flutter of excitement. It was piloted by an officer who had come to witness Mr Hucks' exhibition. Its passage over the city attracted a great deal of attention.'

In July 1914 aircraft from Yarmouth flew down to Spithead on the Solent to participate in the annual Naval Review. Based at the naval air station at Calshot, they flew over the fleet review, including a flight at night with the whole fleet lit up. It was while at Calshot, Reggie later recalled, that the naval airmen were first told that the Naval Wing of the Royal Flying Corps was to separate and become the Royal Naval Air Service. On the return flight to Yarmouth Reggie suffered his last crash before the outbreak of war. The Whitstable local newspaper reported:

9

A Naval airman, Lieutenant Reginald J Bone, with Mr Henry, a wireless operator, was proceeding in naval waterplane (no. 141) from Calshot, Southampton to the Isle of Grain air station and when about a mile and a half off Tankerton was planning down when, not knowing he was so close to the water owing to the glare of the sun light misleading him, the water plane struck the water with such force that it turned over and was completely wrecked. Before the catastrophe the Naval Lieutenant was flying at only ten or twelve feet above the water, but thinking he was higher he did not turn off his engine. The Lieutenant and his passenger were under the water quite long enough, according to an eye witness of the occurrence, but they came up safely and were rescued by a row boat from one of the yawls. The naval waterplane No. 77, which was a short distance away, came up and Lieut. Bone and Mr Henry were transferred to this and the waterplane brought them on to the beach at Tankerton. Naturally the greatest excitement prevailed among the hut occupiers and others on the beach and soon a large crowd assembled, only to be swelled to greater proportions as the news spread throughout the town. Lieut Bone sprained his ankle and bruised his knee in the fall, but his companion escaped unhurt. Dr Etheridge attended to the Lieutenant, who later lunched at the residence of Dr and Mrs Etheridge.

While Reggie was being entertained by the doctor, the plane was towed ashore. A torpedo boat from Sheerness sent seamen ashore to remove the wireless and other valuable items immediately. The machine was guarded overnight by the police, which didn't prevent spectators from making off with parts of the wreckage. Attempts to get one of the wings away provoked great amusement among spectators as the four sailors trying to carry it fell over several times in the mud. Eventually, the important parts of the wreck were taken away in the torpedo boat the next day.

On his return to Yarmouth Reggie flew patrols along the east coast, including a short spell at Killingholme where his was the only aircraft to defend the oil tanks there against possible Zeppelin attack – which fortunately never materialised. It's also likely that he was the officer in charge at Yarmouth when the town was shelled by German cruisers on 3 November 1914. The air station had no serviceable aircraft and was reduced to sending armed sailors to the beach to repulse a possible landing.

Reggie was then posted to *HMS Empress*, a cross-Channel ferry converted to carry seaplanes. The ship was part of a flotilla of three seaplane carriers (the other two were *Engadine* and *Riviera*) detailed to carry out one of the most daring raids of the war. The Admiralty knew the Germans had a Zeppelin station at Cuxhaven on the North Sea coast and on Christmas Eve 1914, accompanied by an escort of destroyers and cruisers of the Harwich Force, the flotilla set out for the German coast. The pilots, including Reggie, had been briefed by their intelligence officer, Erskine Childers (author of the spy novel *The Riddle of the Sands*), and were to fly to Cuxhaven and bomb the sheds and gasholder before flying back over the German naval bases at the mouth of the Jade and Weser rivers for reconnaissance. At dawn the seaplanes were swung into the water, their wings (which had been folded) were opened and fixed, their engines started and one by one they lifted into the air – with two exceptions, one of which was Reggie Bone's Short seaplane No. 122 which suffered complete engine failure! His aircraft was hauled back aboard and *Empress* made way, with the flotilla, towards the rendezvous point with the returning aircraft. Erskine Childers, who did actually fly in the raid, later commented that Reggie was the only pilot who'd studied his plans properly and it was a shame he hadn't been able to take off.

In his memoirs Reggie recalled another raid soon after,

This ship was sent to Dunkirk to take part in some raids designed to give the public confidence which had been shaken by the German advance of 1914. We were despatched to attack some buildings on the landward end of the mole at Zeebrugge but we were told not to go over the target at less than 5,000 feet. When I told Samson I doubted if we could make that altitude his reply was 'That's up to you'. Our four seaplanes became separated on the way by snowstorms. When I approached the Mole at Zeebrugge at about 3,000 feet the AA fire was heavy and accurate. My instrument board was smashed and a piece of hot metal lodged in my handkerchief – worn in the left hand cuff. At this point I must confess that it occurred to me that I was disobeying the ordered height over the target and I turned aside and bombed a tram at Blankenbergh from a low altitude.

The Dutch papers carried a paragraph 24 hours later that I had hit the tram and killed 105 German soldiers. In 1918 when I was on a Commission to Belgium I went to Blankenbergh and got confirmation of this from local people. They even showed me the marks on a train standard which had been made by the splinters of my bomb. On this raid we lost two splendid young-sters, Desmond O'Brien and Tommy Spencer. [The date of the raid was 16 February 1915 and Desmond O'Brien was son of the 14th Baron of Inchinquin, County Clare.]

After this rather disastrous affair I was transferred to No. 2 Wing RNAS which was forming at Eastchurch under Courtney. It was a strenuous period since the senior officers were doing dual (instruction) all day and had to stand by to pursue Zeppelins – sometimes into the early hours of the morning. The Government were alarmed at the effect on the public of our failure to check these raids and were anxious to have some sort of communique to issue e.g. 'our pilots went up in pursuit etc'. The difficulty was that the Zeppelins could rise quickly to a height that most defending aircraft could not reach . . . At Eastchurch we had some old BE 2c and our weapon was to carry French incendiary darts called 'Fleches' which had to be dropped on the Zeppelin from above. One night a Zeppelin was reported over Dover steering towards Sheerness and two of us – Pierse and myself – went up in pursuit. After patrolling for about two hours over Sheerness and having seen nothing we both returned to

Flight Lieutenant Reggie Bone at Dunkirk, early 1915. (Courtesy of Mrs Rosemary Horrell)

Eastchurch. It must be remembered that we had no radio to give us information; as I approached the flare path I saw Pierse landing alongside it – not on it. For no particular reason I did the same thing. We were both lucky because the Zepp had passed over Eastchurch while we were on patrol and had dropped a very large bomb accurately onto the flare path making an enormous crater. Had we landed on the flare path we should have crashed into this crater.

Shortly after this episode I took one of the squadrons of No. 2 Wing, Dunkirk. We operated against targets at Zeebrugge and behind Ostend and against airship sheds in Belgium – near Brussels. On one occasion my squadron was detailed to attack an airship shed at Gontrode. Two were twin engined pusher Caudrons and the third was my Nieuport. Just before departure I discovered that one of the Caudrons had no machine gun and so I gave him the one from my Nieuport. Shortly after take-off I found myself over Dixmude with two German aircraft at my level and one above. This was an awkward situation so I attacked one of the Germans at my level and he went vertically down in a cloud of exhaust smoke because he was terrified of a Nieuport. I then went out to sea between Nieuport and Ostend – crossed over the Dutch frontier behind Zeebrugge – bombed the airship shed at Gontrode and set my nose for home. Flying into the setting sun I found that I could not see my compass at all. I was forced to steer by the setting sun. My detour via the Dutch frontier had made me very short of petrol and I was delighted to find myself over the canal that runs out at Nieuport. My engine stopped dead within a few

A flight of French-built Caudron two-seater bombers at Dunkirk, 1915. Reggie commanded a mixed flight of Caudrons and Nieuport fighters. (Courtesy of Mrs Rosemary Horrell)

French-built Nieuport fighters at Dunkirk, 1915. Note the Lewis gun on the top wing fixed to fire over the propeller. It was in an aircraft like this Reggie won his DSO.
(Courtesy of Mrs Rosemary Horrell)

moments and I force landed on the beach 2 miles behind Nieuport. Arthur Longmore, who was in command of the RNAS at Dunkirk came out with the party bringing me petrol.

After his period at Dunkirk, Reggie was appointed to command a tiny new station at Detling, just outside Maidstone. German air raids against the Kent coast had become an unfortunate feature of the war and until now the defences had appeared incapable of protecting the coastal towns. On 19 March 1916 Reggie became, at least momentarily, quite a celebrity, as he recalled in his memoirs,

At this time German aircraft were making daylight raids on our east coast towns – there was no radar to give warning of their approach and they did not remain any length of time over their targets and were off to sea again before any defending aircraft could get near them. Due to my experience at Dunkirk I felt that Sunday at lunch time was a probable moment for an attack. I therefore got some sandwiches and a thermos of coffee and flew from Detling to Westgate-on-Sea where we had a small RNAS airfield. I then got my Nieuport lined up into wind and was eating my lunch when some German aircraft bombed

14

the town of Margate close by. My engine was quickly started and I set off in pursuit. The problem was to keep a German aircraft in sight since my climbing speed was only just above their cruising speed. However I managed to do this although it took me a long way towards Zeebrugge before I got up to the height. Finally I got up under his tail and fired a good burst – at which he went down in an almost vertical dive. I saw the seaplane alight and he eventually taxied back to Zeebrugge. The pilot was employed after the war in Deutsch Hansa and he told me that he was hit in the ankle. This was the first time that any British aircraft had made contact with a raiding German aircraft . . . the authorities were so glad to have a Communique that they awarded me an immediate DSO, which I probably did not deserve.

Deserved or not, a tremendous fuss was made of Reggie's success. The *Isle of Thanet Gazette* reported (and mistakenly that he'd been born in Thanet) that on his landing he was cheered by assembled naval and military men, joined by local civilians. He was cheered again when he left Westgate by car to go to a local hotel. On the Monday evening following his fight he and a group of RNAS colleagues attended a performance at the Maidstone Palace Theatre where he was recognised and received an ovation from the audience.

The raid had been the largest so far, with six German seaplanes bombing Dover, Deal, Margate and Ramsgate. Dover and Deal were bombed before the defending aircraft were even aware an attack was taking place and three seaplanes dropped a total of thirty-three bombs on the towns. Just 10 minutes later, at 2.10pm, three more seaplanes attacked Ramsgate and Margate, dropping fifteen bombs. The aircraft Reggie Bone eventually intercepted was one that had bombed Deal, a Freidrichshafen FF 33b from Zeebrugge. The crew sustained minor injuries and the seaplane was eventually towed home. Reggie's official report said that he had made a diving attack from the rear, under fire from the observer, made a second pass in which he thought he'd wounded the observer and then closed in to 20ft firing a series of short bursts until the machine went into a steep dive with the engine smoking.

Though the other defenders (some thirty aircraft took off) didn't make contact, a RFC aircraft, which was crossing the Channel, got on

A posed photograph, taken after he won his DSO, which appeared in several magazines and histories. (Author's Collection)

the tail of another seaplane and forced it down badly damaged. News of this success didn't reach Britain until next day so Reggie, quite unwittingly, made all the headlines. Given that the Germans had killed fourteen people (including four children on their way to Sunday school) and injured twenty-six, the authorities desperately needed good news and Reggie provided it. All the local papers reported his success, as did the national press – including the mass-circulation *Daily Mirror*, which had his photograph on the front page.

Reggie Bone's Later Career

Following his DSO Reggie worked as a test pilot, commanded South Shields Seaplane Station then was posted to the RNAS in the Aegean, commanding B Squadron, then the Mudros Repair Base. Returning to London in late 1917, he was Liaison Officer between the Air Ministry and the RAF in the Aegean. In April 1919, he was CO of the RAF Contingent on HMS *Nairana* in Russia , eventually commanding the whole RAF Contingent of Syrenforce (see Guy Blampied, Chapter 3).

After six months as RAF Liaison Officer with the Government Code and Cypher School advising on RAF ciphers, he was attached to HQ of 3 Group at Grantham then served two years as Director of RAF Recruiting, being involved when Lawrence of Arabia tried enlisting as an aircraftsman under a false name. From 1923 to 1925 he commanded the flying boat base, RAF Calshot, on the Solent. He then went to India, commanding the RAF Depot at Drigh Road, with responsibility for maintaining all RAF machinery in India. Here he again encountered Lawrence of Arabia, who worked in the stores and wrote malicious letters about him to London. Promoted to group captain in 1929, he became Air Attaché in Paris. Having flown the Channel on the same evening as the airship R101, he inspected the burnt out wreckage after it crashed near Paris and identified the hideously burned bodies of his good friend Sefton Brancker, Minister of Civil Aviation, and other officers he'd known. Retiring in 1934, he worked as a civilian in the Air Ministry, then became Director of Civil Aviation to the Egyptian Government. Recalled to the RAF in September 1939, he was Station Commander, RAF Pembroke Dock, finally retiring in 1941. Until 1945 he was RAF Liaison Officer with Civil Defence in the Midlands.

In Birmingham he married a young widow whose husband had been killed on ARP duties, 'inheriting' her small family. He was Civil Aviation Attaché in the Far East in the late 1940s and later worked on jet engines at Lucas Engineering. He died in 1972.

Researching Reggie Bone

Though Reggie wrote his memoirs in later life, his account is very patchy in terms of exact details of his career and some bits one might expect to have been mentioned aren't – there's no reference to his abortive part in the Cuxhaven raid, for example. Dates are rarely given – and are sometimes wrong when they are! If nothing else, this proves all memoirs should be treated with a certain amount of caution and checked and verified with other sources. I also had to piece the story together from rough drafts, typescripts and correspondence.

With such a long and interesting career the sources to be used are many and varied. Some are available online, for example, his *Who's Who* entry is at http://www.ukwhoswho.com/view/article/ oupww/whowaswho/U152445/BONE_Group_Captain_Reginald _John?index=1&results=QuicksearchResults&query=0, which gives basic details of his career. His RN service record covering his service between 1903 and 1919 is in ADM 196 series at TNA and can be searched for and downloaded via the Discovery facility on the TNA website. There is a brief obituary in *The Times* (the digital archive can usually be accessed free via your local libraries website) and there are occasional other references to him in its pages. The *London Gazette* gives details of his appointments, promotions and awards. As an early aviator many of his flights are recorded in *Flight* magazine, available at http://www.flightglobal.com/pdfarchive/ index.html, and it also includes references to other points in his career and has the occasional photograph.

Because of the novelty and popularity of flying in its early years the local press often mentioned incidents of note and the local newspapers for Margate, Maidstone, Great Yarmouth and Eastbourne all contain references to him. Thus far these are only available at either the local record office or library or the British Library newspaper collection at Colindale. Hopefully, these papers will be via the Internet in the near future as part of the British Library's programme of putting newspapers online. The award of Reggie's DSO made all the national press, including a front-page spread in the *Daily Mirror*, which also featured a photograph.

Reggie's RAF service record, since he served after 1919, is retained by the RAF and held at RAF Cranwell. I have a copy as I received his next of kin's authority to access it in the early 1990s, but it should be available to members of the public, with some deletions, provided it can be proved he died more than twenty-five years ago (a copy of his obituary in *The Times* is actually on the file).

Most other records are available at TNA in Kew. There are brief details of his RNAS career in ADM 273/3/21 and ADM 273/31/69. Details of his work in the RNAS and early RAF, up to the end of 1919, are in AIR 1 series, which is a huge and complex series but contains almost all surviving aviation papers from the First World War and before.

The IWM has some of the papers of Erskine Childers, including his well-written and informative diary, which proved invaluable for checking details of Reggie's time on HMS *Empress* and his abortive part in the Cuxhaven raid.

Because of his wide and varied service and reasonably high rank, Reggie is mentioned frequently in books and magazines, though not always by name. As the CO he is referred to in the letters of T E Lawrence covering his time at RAF Drigh Road. There's an account of his shooting down the German seaplane in *The Air Defence of Great Britain* by Christopher Cole and E F Cheesman (Putnam, 1984). He is mentioned, though not by name, in W E Johns' memoirs when he describes the enlistment of T E Lawrence into the RAF at the Henrietta Street Recruiting Office in 1922.

Chapter 2

A MILITARY MEDAL WITH THE ROYAL FLYING CORPS – DAVID PROSSER HEPBURN

D avid Prosser Hepburn was born in 1885 in the Carluker area of Lanarkshire, the third of nine children. It's known that he attended Edinburgh University, studying chemistry, and, presumably while there, served in the 4th Volunteer Battalion, Royal Scots, otherwise known as the Edinburgh Rifles, a rather select (at least as far as its officers went) volunteer unit. The unit had originally been formed, in 1867, as a corps of 'total abstainers', which may help explain David's known almost total abstinence from drink in later life.

When he enlisted, on 28 January 1916 (the date suggests he volunteered), he gave his occupation as chemist which may have been a factor in his joining the Royal Flying Corps as a rigger, those ground crew who worked on the body of the aircraft. Many riggers had previous trades in woodwork, wiring and upholstery (necessary skills when working with canvas and wooden aircraft held together with wire), but riggers were also responsible for painting and doping (applying the hardener to the canvas) so a knowledge of chemistry could be useful. Alongside the riggers worked the fitters, men with mechanical skill who were responsible for the engines, guns and other mechanisms.

Basic military training would have been carried out at Farnborough, long-time home of the RFC with trade instruction given there at the same time. The syllabus for the slightly later school for riggers and fitters at Reading shows that riggers were given instruction on all the RFC aircraft of the time.

Following training, he was posted to the newly forming

19

David Hepburn looking very smart in his RFC 'maternity' jacket; the front flap covered the buttons to prevent them getting caught in machinery. He isn't yet wearing his MM ribbon, suggesting this photograph was taken earlier in 1916. (Courtesy of Andrew Salmond Smith)

70 Squadron, which was destined to go to France to take part in the air fighting over the Battle of the Somme in the summer and autumn of 1916. The squadron was being sent to France specifically to deal with the single-seater Fokker monoplane fighter, which, with its new interrupter gear allowing the pilot to fire his machine gun through his propeller, was causing heavy casualties to the RFC squadrons over the Somme battlefields. They were to be equipped with the brand new Sopwith 1½ Strutter, which had the new interrupter gear allowing its own Vickers machine gun to fire forward, as well as a Lewis gun for the observer.

Alan Bott, who served as an observer with the squadron, later described the confusion that surrounded the move to France in his book *An Airman's Outings with the RFC June – December 1916*. Though written from the point of view of a young officer, it reflects the delays and confusions that must have affected the whole squadron. It's also clear that Bott changed the dates, much in the way that he changed the names of individuals and places.

June opens with an overhaul of officers and men. Last leave is distributed, the doctor examines everybody by batches, backward warriors are worried until they become expert, the sergeant-major polished the men on the grindstone of discipline, the C.O. indents for a draft to complete establishment, an inspection is held by an awesome general. Except for the mobilisation stores everything is complete by June 10.

But there is still no sign of the wanted stores on the Date, and June 16 finds the unit still in the same blinking hole, wherever that may be the days drag on, and Date the second is placed on a pedestal. . . . The Adjutant, light duty, is replaced by an adjutant, general service. Mobilisation stores begin to trickle into the quartermaster's reservoir. But on June 27 the stores are far from ready, and July 6 is miraged as the next Date. This time it looks like business. The war equipment is completed, except for the identity discs. On July 4 a large detachment departs, after 12 hours notice, to replace casualties in France. Those remaining in the now incomplete unit grow wearily sarcastic. More last leave is granted. The camp is given over to rumour . . .

A band of strangers report in place of the draft that went to France, and in them the NCO's plant esprit de corps and the fear of God. The missing identity discs arrive, and a fourth Date is fixed July 21. And the dwellers in the blinking hole, having been wolfed several times, are sceptical, and treat the latest report as a bad joke. 'My dear man,' remarks the subaltern-who-knows, 'it's only more hot air. I never believed in the other dates, and I don't believe in this. If there's one day of the three hundred and sixty-five when we shan't go, it's July the twenty-first.'

And at dawn on July 21 the battalion, battery, or squadron moves unobtrusively to a port of embarkation for France.

The officers of 70 Squadron were hand-picked, because the Sopwith 1½ Strutter was a new aircraft and the best two-seater available at the time. The ground crew were good too; Bott describes them as 'highly trained and the mechanics have already learned their separate trades as riggers, fitters, carpenters, sailmakers and the like . . . the quality of their skilled work is tempered by the technical sergeant-major, who knows most things about an aeroplane and the quality of their behaviour by the disciplinary sergeant-major, usually an ex-regular with a lively talent for blasting'.

A nucleus flight under Captain Cruickshank left Farnborough on 21 May and flew to Fienvillers via St Omer, followed by B Flight under Captain Sanday which arrived on 26 June, followed by C Flight under Captain Salmond on 30 July.

David Hepburn embarked for France on 19 June 1916 and on arrival in France was presumably assigned to B Flight. The aerodrome at Fienvillers was just north of the River Somme, 16 miles east of Abbeville, on 24 June 1916. The squadron was commanded by Major G A K Lawrence DSO, MC, described by Captain Sanday as 'one of the brightest of personalities, admired, respected and beloved by every officer and man'.

A brief history of the squadron in 1916 by Lt Colonel W D S Sanday describes the fighting,

> Heavy reconnaissance work started immediately, with daily offensive patrols of 3½ hours duration, and this work was carried out during the whole battle of the Somme. The two Flights, A and B, carried out all the Army reconnaissance work during July and August, working East to Mons, Maubeuge, Hirson, Basigny etc, and offensive patrols East of Louai and Cambrai.
>
> Heavy fighting took place throughout the whole battle, and although the Squadron had nearly 100 casualties, the Hun aviators were kept well behind their lines. At no period, since or before, were they so noticeably under control. It was a rare occurrence to see a hostile machine on our side of the lines.

The whole concept of keeping the RFC on the offensive, in the face of mounting casualties, was controversial, but the aim was simple: to keep enemy aircraft well behind their lines and so unable to watch the build-up of Allied troops pending offensives on the ground and to keep their artillery from having accurate spotting. Though casualties were high, particularly among new pilots, it does appear to have worked. The high rate of casualties also seems to have been accepted among the officers who fought and flew, as evidenced by Captain Sanday's recollections,

> In A Flight, Capt Manley, with Lt Saint, was severely wounded near Cambrai, early in July, but managed to return to his aerodrome. He was a very gallant young officer, who met his death in a collision in the air in the summer of 1917, while serving with 19 Squadron.
>
> B Flight started their first reconnaissance with bad luck, Capt Veitch and Lt Whitty getting a direct hit from an 'archie' just

east of Arras. It was a very cloudy day and the journey had to be made at a very low altitude. Capt Sanday and Lt Hilmore reached Cambrai and obtained a very successful report, although Capt Sanday was wounded by shrapnel in the ankle, while flying at 2,000 feet over the town.

During the month of July, the Germans appeared to be afraid of the Sopwiths, and only put heart into their attacks when they could separate a machine from the others.

Up until the end of September B Flight was fortunate to lose only three aircraft, in part because it kept formation well so that its machine guns could offer mutual support. Two aircraft were lost due to direct hits from German anti-aircraft artillery and one, flown by Lieutenant Blain with Lieutenant Griffiths as observer, suffered engine failure and came down behind German lines. Both officers were captured, but, after three attempts, Blain managed to escape, only to be killed later in an accident at RAF Martlesham Heath.

C Flight came out to France in August with Captain Salmond, who was shot down and captured shortly afterwards. Command of the flight was taken over by Captain Cochrane Patrick, who had two observers killed while flying with him on successive days.

According to another brief history of 70 Squadron, between May and October 1916 the squadron lost 14 pilots and 14 observers recorded as missing, 7 pilots and 5 observers wounded and 6 observers killed. It claimed 40 enemy aircraft brought down.

On 9 September Sopwith two-seater No. A/1911, flown by 2nd Lieutenant E J Henderson with 2nd Lieutenant G N Cousans as observer, took off to fly an offensive patrol over the Bapaume–Fins–Bois de Bourlon sector of the front. Close to the French lines just south of the River Somme itself the aircraft was ambushed by three German aircraft and hit through the petrol tank; Lieutenant Henderson was forced to make a crash landing close to the lines. Lieutenant Cousans was killed but Henderson was able to reach the French lines and was returned to the squadron. The combat report he submitted reads,

Presumably three H.A. dived down from above and behind. Burst of fire from first machine shot through aileron control and petrol tank, stopping the engine. Fire from second machine killed the observer who was retaliating, firing upwards about

8 shots. Machine gliding down with the wind, third H.A. fired into it from above again. A few shots fired from underneath by H.A. Machine glided over French lines shot at from enemy trenches, and landed in French lines about ½ mile behind front line trench at 5.20 p.m. at Soyecourt. Crashed machine owing to lack of right aileron control. Got observer into trench 10 yards away and he was pronounced dead by French Medical Corps. Went to Brigade Hdqrs to telephone, and was not allowed to go back to machine for an hour. Got back to the machine and removed Lewis gun. Walked back to Foucancourt and thence to Divisional & Army Corps Hdqrs.

A handwritten note from Major Lawrence, the Squadron Commanding Officer, was added two days later,

2nd Lt Henderson, having telephoned his information, returned to the machine, which was in an exposed position, in the dark and removed the Lewis gun and Very pistol. He endeavoured to remove the Vickers gun but could not do so owing to lack of tools. He carried the gun and pistol back to a dug out near FRAMERVILLE and here he slept in the field.

The aircraft had come down close to the lines near the village of Soyecourt, a couple of miles south of the River Somme, in a sector that had only been captured by the French in an advance a few days

A French postcard showing the French trenches at Soyecourt, probably taken about the time David Hepburn was there recovering the aircraft.

before. The trench line lay along the edge of the village and the Germans had pulled back to a new line across a shallow valley about half a mile to the east.

Though the squadron had lost other aircraft, some of them behind German lines, the Sopwith was a new aircraft with valuable new technology, including the interrupter gear. The next day a group of airmen, including David, was sent from the airfield to try and salvage the remains of the aircraft. One of the few stories that the family has from David was that enemy shrapnel bounced off the roof of the tender lorry that he and his comrades were despatched in to attempt the recovery. Crawling out from the French trenches and under fire from snipers and mortars, they made several trips and were able to bring back most of the important (and expensive) parts of the wreckage. The whole group were recommended for the Military Medal, the recommendation reading,

On 10th September 1916 these NCO's and air mechanics were sent to SOYECOURT in the French line to salve a wrecked machine which lay in the open 800 yards from the front line, in view of the German trenches.

By working all day on the machine they salvaged the whole lot of it, making six journeys across 400 yards of open ground (to where the machine was left).

e No.	Unit	Regtl. No.	Rank and Name	Action for which commended	Recommended by	Honour or Reward	C
			Brigade. 9th WING.	Division. ROYAL FLYING Corps. 9th October 1916.	Date of Recommendat		
	70 Squadron R.F.C.	S.R.7	Corporal Charles WILLS.	On 10th September 1916 these N.C.O's and air mechanics were sent to SOYECOURT in the French line to salve a wrecked machine which lay in the open 800 yards from the front line, in view of the German trenches.		Military Medal	
	70 Squadron R.F.C.	17518	1st Class Air Mechanic (Acting Corporal) Frederick FROOM.			"	
	70 Squadron R.F.C.	19101	1st Class Air Mechanic Leonard Charles ROBERTS.	By working all day on the machine they salved the whole of it, making six journeys across a mile of open ground to where the car was left.		"	
	70 Squadron R.F.C.	10720	2nd Class Air Mechanic Benjamin HARRISON.	They wre under intermittent sniping and small trench mortar fire the whole day.		"	
	70 Squadron R.F.C.	19723	2nd Class Air Mechanic David Prosser HEPBURN.	By their resolution and indifference to danger they saved material of considerable value to the government, though the French Military Authorities declared that owing to its position it could not be saved.		"	
	27 Squadron R.F.C.	1739	Acting Sergeant Major Cecil MARLEY.	February to October 1916. Has done excellent work in the Squadron. Salving machine under fire. Has previous service in France.		D.C.M.	

David Hepburn's commendation for his Military Medal, note Hugh Dowding's signature on the right. (TNA AIR 1/1031/204/5/1433)

They were under intermittent sniping and trench mortar fire the whole day.

By their resolution and indifference to danger they saved material of considerable value (to the government, though the French Military Authorities declared that owing to its position it could not be saved).

The recommendation was signed by Lieutenant Colonel H C T Dowding, Commanding 9 Wing RFC, who later went on to head Fight Command during the Battle of Britain.

Though the wreckage was saved the aircraft itself was struck off, the damage to the aircraft consisting of 'All longerons broken. Engine bearers broken. Steel engine bearers badly bent and shot. Undercarriage broken. Three planes wrecked and fourth shot about. Tail plane and elevator shot.', from the RFC report on 'Casualties to Personnel and Machines (When Flying)' in AIR 1/845/204/5/374.

David told his tale to the local newspaper,

A fine young Irish officer was brought down near the French first line and we two went out to get the machine back. We were shelled and sniped all day. The French and German artillery were having a great duel and we were in between. The Huns almost succeeded in blowing up our automobile trailer. They thought they had done us away but we returned to the open at night from our holes in the earth and took the machine away. Two French officers guided us by a road near no man's land.

On 12 September David was transferred to 19 Squadron RFC, also based at Fienvillers. The squadron was flying BE 12 aircraft, single-

A French postcard showing the French trenches at Soyecourt, 1916.

seater tractor aircraft (the propeller was mounted at the front) with 140hp air-cooled engines. They too were armed with a synchronised Vickers machine gun firing forward through the propeller and a Lewis gun mounted to fire backwards; they also mounted bomb racks capable of carrying eight 20lb or two 112lb bombs and carried a camera. Commanded by Major Rodwell, 19 Squadron was also flying in support of the Somme battle which had been raging for over two months. The squadron had only recently suffered terrible losses when, on 26 August, a formation of ten machines had set out to bomb the railway at Havrincourt Wood where German troops were believed to be detraining. Having bombed the railway, the aircraft were returning when they ran into a huge thunder storm that had suddenly got up; finding it impossible to climb above it, they decided to try and fly through it on a compass bearing. The first five machines entered the storm but no sooner had they done so than a strong flight of German aircraft fell on the remainder. In spite of stout resistance, they were overwhelmed and all forced down, two taken prisoner, two killed outright and one more dying while a prisoner of war.

On arrival David was posted to B Flight, commanded by Captain I H D Henderson, with Lieutenants Child, G B A Baker and F C Selous (son of the famous big-game hunter). It was to be the start of a short but intensive period of fighting as the Battle of the Somme moved into its third phase, usually referred to as the Battle of Flers-Courcelette. It was hoped that the first use of tanks (though on a limited scale) would break the German line. Though there were initial advances they didn't make the anticipated breakthrough and the main battle continued as a series of smaller attacks with more limited objectives. The following quotation is taken from 'A Short History of No. 19 (Fighter) Squadron RAF' in AIR 1/689/21/20/19,

> The 15th September, the opening day of the third phase of the Somme battle, was marked by the first appearance of tanks at the front. To specially selected pilots of No 19 Squadron was allotted the task of a continuous and very close patrol low over the trenches, from the time the attack started, in order to report direct every movement of our advance, and, particularly, the position of the tanks. Before dawn on this day the first pilot, Captain Henderson, went up on the special contact patrol. Before he returned another pilot, Second Lieutenant F H B

Selous, was sent to maintain contact with the troops and he in turn was succeeded by Lieutenant G B A Baker. Each pilot as he returned with news was at once driven to RFC HQ and thence to GHQ to report direct. The first machine flown by Captain Henderson came back riddled with bullets and on his return from the second trip, when he reported having seen one of our tanks capture a village at the head of a column of men, several wires and struts of his machine had been shot through and his engine damaged by a bullet. During the few days the push lasted neither pilots nor machines were spared. In addition to the contact patrols, the squadron continued its offensive patrols and bombing, and in order to keep pace with the demand for machines the personnel worked night and day shifts for the repair of those aeroplanes damaged by AA and machine gun fire.

As long as the push lasted and the weather held, these operations were continued night and day and everyone worked at their highest pressure. The strain on the NCOs and mechanics was very heavy. There was the handling of the machines, the starting up of their engines . . . and the fitting of bombs and guns. More than at any other time were machines damaged by anti-aircraft and other gun fire, and so badly were they needed that they had to be repaired at once without waiting until others could be delivered. This meant working night and day shifts, with several men on both. To this was added the night flying, which called for more time and energy from those on the ground than any other operations. Any man was lucky who obtained a full night's rest during the four days following the 15th.

The BE 12 was not the best aircraft to be fighting against faster and better armed German fighters, so in November 1916 the squadron was re-equipped with the SPAD aircraft, described in one history as 'the fastest scout in the air'. The Spad VII had a 150hp Hispano Suiza engine and was a single-seater fighter armed with a synchronised Vickers machine gun that had already seen service with the French air service. The first SPAD arrived in early October and by December the squadron had six machines. All the officers were sent on special courses at St Omer and to the new Aerial Musketry Range at Camiers. Presumably, the riggers and fitters also undertook instruction in working with the new aircraft. According to one history, 'although occasional line patrols were carried out, test and practice flights on the Spads constituted the main work of the squadron in the first two months of 1917'.

For other ranks such as David the work and day-to-day activities were pretty routine. A schedule from early 1917 gives reveille at 6am, breakfast at 6.45am, parade with belts, pistols and ammunition pouches at 7.30am, dinner at 12.15pm, parade for work (NCOs and men under the rank of flight sergeant to parade in jean combinations) at 2pm, tea at 5pm, guard mounting at 6.30pm, roll call at 9pm and lights out at 9.15pm. Work after tea when necessary and as ordered. Parade in marching order at 7.30am first and third Sunday in the month.

On 20 February 1917 David, who the family believe could speak French, along with another rigger, Corporal Tizard, was posted to Paris as part of the British Aeronautical Supplies Department.

The British Aeronautical Supplies Department, based in Paris, had formerly been known as the British Aviation Commission, a joint War Office and Admiralty purchasing commission for buying French aircraft and equipment. On 1 January 1917 it had been taken over by the Ministry of Munitions but the military officers and men serving in it remained on the strength of the British Expeditionary Force.

Little is known about David's individual service with the BASD; his service record shows him as having been admitted to the Detention Hospital, Paris, with a sprained ankle on 4 May 1917 and being discharged six days later. He also had a short spell in the 8th Canadian General Hospital in August 1918 suffering from diarrhoea. According to his son William, he was, at one stage, affected by an outbreak of fleas or some other insect that broke out among the men, but was cured by the application of 'Tue Tout' ('kills all'), a French patent medicine he obtained from a pharmacy. His family, rather tantalisingly, seem to think that because of his fluent French he was employed clandestinely at some point actually spying on Frenchmen suspected of spying for the Germans, but there is nothing I've been able to find as yet to confirm this. Probably, the bulk of his work remained of a technical nature, checking the quality of purchases, though there were a few aircraft based in the Paris area and he may have worked on those.

According to his son, he went home to Scotland in 1919 to marry, but was not sent back to Paris and was discharged from the RAF while at home; certainly this latter is borne out by his service record which shows that he was transferred to the RAF Reserve on 15 February 1919 and finally discharged fully on 30 April 1920. He married Margaret Dunn and they had four children: David Prosser, William Dunn, Margaret Prosser and Helen. He went on to become a teacher and eventually headmaster of Muirhead School in Uddingston, near Glasgow.

Researching David Prosser – Service Records Never Lie?

At the start of the research into David Prosser there was not much information to go on: a photograph of him in RFC uniform showing that he was an 'other rank' and his name. At one point his grandson had owned a newspaper clipping saying that he'd been awarded a Military Medal for salvaging an aircraft under fire, but this had been lost. Fortunately, a relative was able to locate their copy in the course of the research.

Records for RFC (and later RAF) other ranks are held in ledgers in TNA series AIR 79. They're not available online and are in service number order but a recent (and most welcome) exercise by the staff at TNA has indexed the entire series by the name that appears on the service record. David Hepburn's is indexed under his full name of David Prosser Hepburn and the reference is AIR 79/213/19723. The document is AIR 79/213 (this is what you'd request on TNA's system) and 19723 is his service number within the file. Please note that AIR 79 contains the records of virtually all First World War airmen with the exception of men who became officers, continued to serve after the mid-1920s or (in the case of a few men who served with RFC Balloon Units) were transferred back into the army. There are even service records for men who were killed during the war.

The *London Gazette* is the Government's official newspaper, published daily, which records, among other things, the award of medals. It would undoubtedly have recorded (gazetted) the award of a Military Medal to David Prosser. The *London Gazette* is available online at http://www.london-gazette.co.uk and has a search facility for locating records. It has to be said that this is a temperamental facility and quite a degree of patience and experimentation are necessary to find any useful information. It does help sometimes if you have a service number as the system recognises numbers better that it recognises names. In David's case I eventually found him by searching on D P Hepburn and the gazette date was 9 December 1916. Using this as a cut-off date and searching AIR 1 for honours and awards in the year 1916 I located his recommendation in AIR 1/1031/204/5/1433 'Honours and Awards 1916 Mar – 1918 Dec'. Though I was lucky, and hit the right file fairly quickly, there are fifteen files with 'Honours and Awards' in the title for 1916 alone, so it could have been a long search.

David Prosser's service record seemed clear-cut; he transferred to 19 Squadron on 12 September 1916 and stayed with them until late 1918, when he was transferred to an unspecified unit in Paris. Normally, one wouldn't query a service record but 19 Squadron records are remarkably complete, unlike many similar squadrons. The squadron record books survive in AIR 1 (between AIR 1/1486/204/37/1 and AIR 1/1488/204/37/12).

The record books confirmed David's posting to 19 Squadron and that on arrival he was posted to B Flight and confirmed the date that his Military Medal was awarded, so it seemed reasonable to check the date that his service record said he was posted to Paris (without saying to which unit), 5 September 1918. To my surprise there was no reference to this on or around the date in question, nor could I find mention of his periods in hospital, even though other airmen's hospitalisations were clearly recorded. In a situation like this there is, unfortunately, only one course of action – to plough through the record books until something pops up; luckily, in this case, it was relatively early as on 20 February 1917 the record book states:

> The undermentioned having proceeded to 2 AD on transfer to BASD Paris 20/02/17 are struck off the strength of No 19 Squadron with effect from that date
> No 8292 Cpl Tizard S Rigger
> No 19723 1 A/M Hepburn DS Rigger

On examination of a number of AIR 79 records it becomes clear that they are not 'original' records but were compiled retrospectively by the RAF after the war, from original RFC documentation that was, presumably, destroyed. Any gaps or errors in the record, should they occur, have to be filled from other sources. Corporal Tizard's service record erroneously says that he was first posted to BASD on 22 July 1917 but the squadron Operational Record Book (ORB) says it was on 20 February.

The remains of the French trenches at Soyecourt as they are today. (Author's photograph)

Records for the BASD (which are mainly about either officers' pay and allowances or amount of equipment purchased) are either in AIR 1 or in MUN series but give little information about day-to-day activities or the work of individuals.

Though most of the Somme trenches were filled in again after the war, by luck a section of them remained in private hands on the edge of Soyecourt village. Though badly neglected, so that all that remain are lines of what appear to be deep ditches surrounded by circular depressions, all overgrown with trees and shrubs, they are still there. They were donated to the French nation by their owner as the Bois de Wallieux in 1998. Some explanatory boards in French and English explain the context and history of the site and paths allow you to walk around it. Photographs show what the trenches looked like in 1916 and it's possible to walk out into what was no-man's-land to get some small idea of what it must have been like for David Hepburn as he crawled out to recover the aeroplane and win his Military Medal.

Chapter 3

AIR WAR IN THE ARCTIC CIRCLE – BERTRAM GUY BLAMPIED

Bertram Guy Blampied (generally known as Guy) was born on Guernsey on 17 December 1899. Initially educated at Elizabeth College, Guernsey, he was a pupil at Queen's College, Taunton, between September 1911 and Easter 1917, and became a sergeant major in their Officer Cadet Corps. He volunteered for the RNAS and was posted first to the Royal Naval College at Greenwich for his basic officer training then to Vendôme in France for his basic flying training. He transferred to the RAF on 1 April 1918 when the RNAS and RFC merged to form the new service. He saw service on the seaplane carrier HMS *Campania* with the Grand Fleet and at the RAF station at Torquay before he was posted to the ship that was to take him to fight in one of the RAF's more curious small wars.

Guy joined HMS *Nairana* in the Firth of Forth on 11 March 1919 and in early May was sent, along with the other pilots, to the Isle of Grain in Kent for flying training. *Nairana* was loaded with stores and four Fairey 3c seaplanes and sailed for Murmansk, in north Russia, arriving there on 28 May.

The campaign Guy was to fly and fight in was a peculiar one. Following the Russian Revolution in 1917, and particularly after Russia signed a peace treaty with Germany in March 1918, Britain had been concerned that Germany might seize the huge stocks of war material that had built up at the Russian ports of Murmansk and Archangel. With the initial approval of the Bolshevik government, British troops had landed in Murmansk in March 1918 but relations had deteriorated and by August 1918, when British and

33

Allied troops forcibly seized Archangel, Britain and Russia were virtually at war. The armistice with Germany in November 1918 came too late for there to be any consideration of withdrawing Allied troops; the White Sea was frozen over completely and troops were dug in over 100 miles from the ports in Archangel and Murmansk with no chance of getting away. The troops hung on through an arctic winter and in the spring of 1919 plans were laid to get them out. This involved sending out a relief force that would hold the line and allow the troops to be withdrawn. The political situation had developed over the winter and Russia was now in the grip of a vicious civil war between the Bolshevik (Red) government in Moscow and disparate groups of 'White' Russians, including a White government at Archangel. Inevitably, perhaps, the relief force was seen as intervening in the civil war and this was encouraged by elements within the British Government, particularly Winston Churchill and Lord Curzon. It was finally decided that the relief force would, itself, be withdrawn in September 1919 and, in the meantime, White Russian forces would be recruited and trained to take over from them.

It was a campaign fought in thickly forested country with few roads, tracks, towns or even villages. Maps, where they existed, proved to be highly inaccurate. As well as the country, the RAF Contingent had to contend with extremes of temperature and, as much of the fighting was close to, or within, the Arctic Circle, continuous 24-hour daylight. Many flights that took off in what one might expect to be hours of darkness flew in daylight equivalent to late afternoon in Britain.

Guy Blampied, having bathed in Lake Onega, stands in front of his Fairey 3c seaplane No. N9235. (Courtesy of Guy Blampied)

34

On their arrival at Murmansk the RAF men were told that they were to proceed, by a single-track railway, to support a recent advance by the army which had pushed forward to the shores of Lake Onega, some 500 miles (by rail) to the south. The spring thaw meant the ice that normally covered the lake was expected to be gone by the end of the first week of June and their seaplanes were urgently needed to deal with the Soviet Lake Flotilla based further south at Petravadosk. Guy's diary takes up the story,

June 2nd: Had a flight in Fairey 3c, our new seaplanes in the morning. Got on alright. Advance party to leave tonight for Lake Onega. Ship came alongside pier at 3.30. Very busy getting stores on shore, and two seaplanes on train. We left Murmansk at midnight, 7 officers and 30 hands.

3rd: Our party, McNab, Harvey, Ross-Smith, Sinclair, Lettington, Smithson & myself. Train arrived at Kola at 1 am and stopped till 5 pm. Went for a walk with Mac in afternoon.

6th: Arrived Medveja Gora at 12 o'clock. The second train arrived at 5 pm. Seaplanes put on siding near beach and we got the first machine in the air at 8 pm. Crowds down to watch.

Fairey 3c N9235 taking off from the beach at Medveja Gora with Guy at the controls.
(Courtesy of Guy Blampied)

Bolshy front line is about 5 miles away. 'A quick job of which we are all very proud'.

7th: Very busy day with flying and settling down. We are still living in the train for the time being.

8th: had reconnaissance flight with Thursfield to Shchunga and district.

Shortly after midnight on the 8/9 June the Soviet Lake Flotilla made its expected appearance, reconnoitring the bay in which the air station was situated. Haines and Eades were on patrol watching for enemy vessels by the light of the midnight sun and they immediately attacked the Russian steamers with a 112lb bomb and three 20lb bombs before being forced to return to Medveja Gora when their Lewis gun jammed. Now alerted, two more aircraft quickly took off, including Guy, piloting N9235, and began to attack the flotilla. They were soon joined by Haines and Eades who had refuelled and rearmed their aircraft and the three seaplanes strafed and bombed the ships, straddling one steamer with two 20lb bombs. Anti-aircraft fire was heavy and accurate, one aircraft being hit just 3in from the observer, but the observer's Lewis guns poured a concentrated fire onto the ships' bridges and their gunners and the flotilla turned and fled south at 10 knots. The small Allied naval flotilla joined the chase and drove the Bolsheviks off. General Maynard, commanding officer of the whole force, later wrote, 'The enemy were seemingly unprepared for attack from the air and no

RAF fitters working on a Fairey 3c seaplane at Medveja Gora. A canvas hangar is being erected on the right and the seaplane station is being built in the background. (Author's Collection)

sooner was the first bomb dropped than they turned about, dispersed and steamed off at full speed.' Guy's diary records, '10th Mac made me officer in charge of beach. Very nice job.'

Over the next few days the RAF Flight made a series of raids on Soviet positions around Siding 10, where it appeared a supply dump was being established. Guy flew five missions in three days, on one occasion scoring a near miss on a moving train with a 230lb bomb, then pursuing it up the line while his observer, Lieutenant Thursfield, strafed it with his Lewis gun. On 11 June Isaac and Eades succeeded in breaking the line by flying along the track at tree-top height and releasing a delayed action fused bomb. From 30ft a 230lb bomb created a 20ft-diameter crater and destroyed a length of track.

While his colleagues continued round the clock patrols and attacks (being close to the Arctic Circle there was nearly 24-hour daylight), Guy was put in charge of a group of prisoners of war as a working party on the beach,

I was put in charge of the beach work and fortunately we were able to get a party of Russian POWs, who were selected as being very anti-bolshevik and wanted to work for us and, indeed, were terribly distressed when we left in September. We used to collect as many as we wanted each day . . . a small party came regularly each day and were put in charge of the larger groups. Later on some of the specially good ones were entrusted with all kinds of work. A Russian POW caused some

The senior Russian prisoners of war who worked under Guy on the seaplane station. (Courtesy of Guy Blampied)

consternation one day when an inspecting Army Officer found him loading Lewis gun ammunition trays. The Russians helped clear the beach and were splendid workmen and very efficient with any woodwork; fortunately we had an unlimited supply of wood. They cleared the site of tree stumps, put down planking, built gantries over the railway lines, put down slip-ways into the water and laid duckboards.

In addition to his work on the beach, Guy flew many missions, only a few of which merited mention in his diary. On 17 June he flew a photo reconnaissance mission with Lieutenant Ross-Smith, the unit's photographer, over the line between Siding 10 and Kapaselga. At 8,000ft they came under anti-aircraft fire which they described in their report as 'Exceptionally inaccurate . . . the shells burst several thousand feet below the machine.' Guy later wrote that,

Our flying duties consisted of bombing, photography and reconnaissance and as it was light all night flying occurred at any time. During June and July the ground staff were hard put to keep the machines flying . . . I flew four different machines until 21st June (I suppose the original four we had in Nairana) and then 2 more 9237 and 9238 appear, I presume from the original equipment sent out with us, and it is not until August when we had large reinforcements that other machines appear. . . . Most of the bombing was done with 230lb and 112lb bombs, the observer frequently took a few 20lb bombs with him to throw over the side.

On 21 June Guy was returning from a raid on Dianovi Gori when his observer, Lieutenant Ross-Smith, spotted seaplane N9238 drifting 7 miles off the shore, having suffered engine failure and descended onto the lake where it was in danger of drifting onto a lee shore. Having alighted nearby, Guy and Lieutenant Ross-Smith were able to throw a line across and towed their colleagues back up the lake until they were relieved of the task by an American motor launch.

On 23 June the main attack was launched against Siding 10 supported by the RAF seaplanes. The station at Siding 10 was attacked with bombs and machine guns and spotting was carried out for the army's artillery. By the 28th Siding 10 had fallen and Allied forces were advancing towards Kapaselga to the south and on the 29th Guy and Ross-Smith bombed the station there with 20lb bombs, cratering the area between the station itself and the track; by 6.30pm they were back at base.

Later in the evening Lieutenants Haines and Eades were in the air south of Kapaselga and spotted a train steaming down the line. Using a refinement of their technique for attacking the line, they flew at tree-top height along the length of the train and, once they got ahead of it, dropped a 230lb bomb with a 2½ second fuse. As the train passed overhead the bomb exploded, demolishing the fuel wagon and leaving the rear half of the engine in the crater with the rest of the engine derailed. At 1am Guy and Lieutenant Harvey were sent to reconnoitre the wreckage. Guy's

Guy's colleagues, Haines (left) and Eades, who destroyed a Soviet train with a bomb. (Courtesy of Guy Blampied)

diary records, 'Went over Kapaselga with Harvey at 2,400 feet and machine was hit by a Bolshy machine gun. Hit in petrol tank and radiator, had to land in trees.' He later wrote a more detailed description of his adventures,

> The shortage of seaplanes was not helped when I was shot down in N9235 on 30th June, on a reconnaissance flight over Kapaselga. I was turned out of bed at about 1 am . . . the wind was blowing on shore so I took straight off and did not gain sufficient height before flying over enemy held forest so I was hit by machine gun fire . . . one petrol tank was holed but I managed to switch to the other and keep the engine going. It

heated up as one radiator had been holed . . . so I had to land in the trees. Neither Lt Harvey my observer nor I were hurt and we walked through the forest heading north (fortunately the sun was up to guide us) and after six hours we reached Lobska Gor. We found a farm . . . saw the farmer and drew a picture of a horse and cart, which he produced and drove us back to camp where we could reward him with plenty of rations.

The diary records: 'July 1st: lay in bed till tea feeling OK but was badly bitten by mosquitos. Major Stewart Dawson and a party (including Harvey) went through the woods to machine to get spares. Party did not stay long as was too close to Bolshys.'

Following Haines and Eades's direct hit enemy trains travelled almost exclusively at night, preventing the rapid movement of Bolshevik reinforcements. The Soviet navy also came in for attention from the RAF when, on 1 July, Lieutenants Lettington and Radford scored a direct hit on a paddle steamer, causing her boilers to explode and her crew to run her ashore.

Over the next few days, according to his diary, Guy was forced to rest, though he had a short flight on the 4 July. On the 7th,

The wreckage of Guy's seaplane being recovered in the forest. (Courtesy of Guy Blampied)

Jimmy Noonan (Rigging Officer), 5 hands and I went up to Siding 9 in evening to get spares. Walked through woods and got to machine at 11.30 (2 hours walk). Mosquitoes very bad. 8th: Left machine at 5.30 am to wait at Siding 9 till 1.30 for train. Went to Kapaselga station and saw hole made by bomb dropped by Ross-Smith and myself – 'Jolly Roger' blew up.

The *Jolly Roger* was the flagship of the Allied naval flotilla, a petrol-driven vessel armed with several machine guns. Her petrol engine exploded, killing five of her crew; fortunately, two RAF seaplanes were able to alight on the water alongside the blazing wreck and the remaining crew jumped overboard and clung to their floats as they taxied ashore. In this way seven men were rescued. The loss of the largest Allied vessel on the lake might have proved a major blow, but this situation was softened by the arrival, by rail, of several Submarine Chasers to make up a new flotilla. Guy's diary records, '12th July: Last night of the old Lake Flotilla. Command now taken by Commander Curtis RN. Had a fine rag, ended by RAF taking all the Lake Flotilla on a cart into the lake at 3 am.'

Guy was still very busy in his role as Beach Officer, particularly as a visit of inspection was scheduled from the Commanding-Officer-in-Chief, General Maynard. '19th July: Not feeling up to much. Doc gave me some pills. GOC is inspecting the unit tomorrow so Bolshys are busy cleaning up. 20th: General Maynard inspected unit at 11 am and was very pleased. Make and Mend for rest of the day. Still rather groggy.' Possibly because of his continuing illness, the Major decided that Guy could do with a spell back on HMS *Nairana* and he was sent by train to the small port of Kem where he rejoined the ship. For a few days at least he enjoyed playing hockey on the quay, pictures in the ship's hangar, boat races and swimming. *Nairana* received instructions to proceed to Archangel to pick up some new aircraft that had been delivered there by the new aircraft carrier HMS *Argus*. Though Guy was specifically told he couldn't accompany *Nairana*, his diary records he 'Wangled out of it' and he sailed with her on 31 July, making the trip in 11 hours, '31st July: Anchored near *Argus*. Had to get 6 Shorts aboard, a difficult job. Managed it finally, put two on the quarter-deck. Went out to *Argus* to get trolleys and turned in at 1.30.'

Next day *Nairana* sailed up the Dvina River to pick up another Short seaplane from a barge, '2nd August: Got one machine off

barge and onto flight-deck. Working all night and up until 3pm. Elope (Archangel) and Syren (Murmansk) stores all mixed up, had to be sorted out. Turned in at 4 o'clock. Ship left for Popoff at 5 pm.' Guy later explained to me that, 'We understood that UK dockers would not load supplies for Russia and it was only when it was known that the force would be withdrawn that supplies were forwarded.'

By August the decision had been made in London that all British personnel were to be withdrawn from north Russia before winter set in. General Rawlinson arrived from London to coordinate the Murmansk and Archangel fronts and brought fresh troops for one final offensive. This, it was planned, would put the Bolsheviks off balance and create a breathing space to allow White Russian troops to take over the front line. New RAF reinforcements also arrived, including Captain Gerry Livock (later Group Captain G E Livock). After some problems with the train (an aircraft being carried became entangled with telegraph wires), Guy and his colleagues arrived back at Medveja Gora at midnight on 4/5 August, '5th August: Found old *Nairana* unit washed out and a Wing started (Seaplanes and Aeroplanes). A rotten affair. Carried on with Ruskies. Cpl Whelan left for ship (Cpl Whelan was the NCO who went to the Russian POW camp to collect however many bolos we wanted for that day).'

During Guy's absence a combined operation with the Lake Flotilla had resulted in the greatest success of the campaign so far for *Nairana's* small detachment. On 3 August an amphibious assault was launched against Tolvoya, a Bolshevik stronghold on the Shunga peninsula, with a column of White Russian partisans advancing down the coast, the Lake Flotilla attacking from the sea and four seaplanes flying in support. The aircraft cornered the Soviet flotilla in Tolvoya harbour, bombing and machine-gunning them until two ran themselves ashore, their crews escaping into the forest, and two tried to run for it, pursued by the seaplanes, before they were eventually captured by the Allied flotilla. At a stroke the main Soviet naval threat in the northern lake had been removed. The captured vessels were pressed into service with the Allies. The largest, the *Silni,* was a 300-ton, twin-screwed steamer mounting two 3in guns, one 3-pounder and six machine guns. A smaller destroyer, with two 3in guns and two machine guns, an armed tug and several barges were also captured. It was a considerable victory and owed much to the professionalism of *Nairana's* pilots and observers.

With the capture of Tolvoya, emphasis shifted to attacks on the main Soviet base further down the lake at Petravadosk, with air raids being made against shipping and the dock facilities. On 7 August Guy flew a bombing mission against the town with Ross-Smith as his observer, who spotted that an important railway bridge over the River Suna, which had previously been damaged, was close to being repaired. Next day Captain Park succeeded in dropping a 230lb bomb on the repaired section and completely wrecked it.

On 9 August Livock was made Commanding Officer of the seaplane flight. Over the next few days reinforcements arrived down the railway, including some aeroplanes to operate from a landing strip carved out of the forest. Among these aircraft were a number of Sopwith Camels and the crates they came packed in were quickly seized by the more-experience pilots and rigged out as accommodation. On 11 August Guy's diary notes, 'Sub and I started rigging out Camel case'; on 12 August he was 'Working on Camel case in spare time'. On 15 August, 'Sub and I slept in the Camel case for the first time. We had rigged the bunks one above the other so as to leave more room.' On the 17th Guy was still working with his Bolshevik prisoners, 'had 100 Bolshy's down at 7'oc to unload a train which had arrived with four Bessaneau hangars'. On the 22nd Guy and his prisoners took down an old hangar and began clearing up to erect the new Bessaneau hangars and next day were cutting down trees to create extra space. He also 'Fixed up old petrol tank and pipes for wash basin in our hut'.

In addition to this work (and not recorded in his diary), Guy flew a reconnaissance and bombing mission against Siding 8 on 17 August and on the 22nd flew two missions over Bolshevik positions around Koi Kori. The Sopwith Camels and other land-based aircraft, originally sent out because of worries about Bolshevik fighters, found themselves without any aerial opposition and spent their time strafing and bombing land targets. The officers who had come out with these aeroplanes were all volunteers (including Lieutenant A Gerrard, who had won a Victoria Cross flying a Camel in Italy), men who were hoping to get a permanent commission in the RAF, which was already being rapidly run down after peace with Germany had been signed. So many men came out that Wing

Commander Bone was obliged to send some home as surplus to requirements.

There was some fraternisation with the local population. Guy later recalled, 'We saw very little of the local population at Medvejya Gora, but I remember a very happy relationship with the Russians at Povonyetz, a town a short way down the lake on the east side which I visited several times in the motor boat.' Diary entry for 1 September: 'Allan, Smith, Livock, Isaac and I went over to Povonyets. Had a fine time. Slept at Martinoffs. Saw Gladys, Shuna and Mora.' The Martinoffs were very friendly with the airmen and their three daughters were certainly a great attraction. Many years later, Livock was to recall, in his autobiography *To the Ends of the Air*, how their meetings, in which communication was only possible through sign language or through an interpreter, were a source of some amusement. On one occasion the interpreter hid behind a curtain while the airmen and girls attempted to converse. When he emerged he threatened to translate all the various asides he'd heard and, to the RAF men's surprise, the girls proved to be even more embarrassed than they were! As the campaign drew to a close and withdrawal became imminent, strenuous efforts were made to persuade the family to evacuate with the Allies, but they preferred to take their chances with the Reds, in spite of the less than veiled threats that were already being made against them.

Guy's diary for 3 September records, 'Langlois crashed the dual Short which was used for instructing the Russkies. Repaired during the night.' One of the tasks of the reinforcements was to train friendly 'White' Russians in flying in the hope of creating a flying corps for the Russian Army that was being left behind. Livock was put in charge of the training flight after a row with Wing Commander Bone about weather conditions prior to a raid, and with the assistance of Lieutenant Isaacs set about trying to instruct ten Russian officers in the handling of seaplanes. Though they were supposed to be pilots already, only one, Lieutenant Korsakoff, appeared to be fully trained. By the time the RAF Contingent was evacuated in late September four of the Russians were considered fully trained, with two more having been instructed as aeroplane pilots by the unit at Lumbushi.

The diary entry for 8 September, 'Flying attack on Koi Kori (failed).' Attacks against Red Army positions at Koi Kori had been being carried out by both aeroplanes and seaplanes for over three weeks by the time Guy mentioned it specifically in his diary. As part of Lord Rawlinson's evacuation scheme it had been agreed with the local White Russian commander, General Skobeltski, that the front line should be pushed forward to the line of the River Nurmis and that flanking columns would seize Koi Kori and Ussuna prior to the handing over of the line. Though, when I asked him, Guy couldn't remember why he'd mentioned that raid specifically it is perhaps more than a coincidence that on the same day there occurred one of the rare occasions of British troops refusing to obey orders, when a battalion of Royal Marines retreated in the face of the enemy. The battalion, which consisted of medically unfit and untried troops, had been diverted to Russia from what they expected to be ceremonial duties in Germany. Rushed up to the front, they ran into an ambush in their first action. A few officers and NCOs fought a desperate rearguard action against a Bolshevik attack, while the men fell back in confusion. The whole battalion was hurriedly sent back to Murmansk, where Court Martial proceedings found many men guilty of mutiny, with sentences ranging from two years' hard labour up to the death penalty for thirteen men. It was only when questions were asked in the House of Commons that sentences were commuted and the men released, having served only a small part of their sentences. No one was executed.

The following diary entries were all made in September:

9th: Maliniski went on his first solo on Short. Got on quite OK. First Russkie to fly solo.

10th: The Russkie CO Col Barbas went solo.

11th: Gen Rawlinson came down to Med. Bone flew him down to Velikaya Guba.

12th: Took M.B. [motor boat] out in evening to test gas bombs which we are to use.

General Rawlinson had located a supply of gas bombs during a visit to Archangel and decided to use them to clear the stiffening Bolshevik resistance being encountered during the final offensive. There is some evidence in files at TNA that its use was not popular among the RAF Contingent – Wing Commander Bone issued a stern order that any orders relating to its use must be strictly adhered to.

A series of raids took place against Lijma, Suna and sidings in the vicinity of Petravadosk, and members of the Russian Flying Corps took part in some of these, mainly flying as observers. Colonel Barbas and Lieutenant Kuschii flew with Park and Maliniski actually flew as pilot, with Lieutenant Allen as observer, to reconnoitre Siding 4. On the whole, however, there was a general feeling among the RAF that the Russians lacked the stomach for real fighting and spent too much time bemoaning 'the good old days'.

Supported by the seaplanes and Camels, which flew numerous missions dropping gas and explosives, the Allied forces pushed south beyond Siding 4 to the line of the River Nurmis and on 18 September began handing over their positions to the White Russians. Only at Koi Kori did they fail to meet their objectives – the heroic resistance that had defeated the Royal Marines was kept up in the face of everything the RAF could deliver.

Accompanied by Livock, Jones and Ross-Smith, Guy made a final visit to Povonyets and the Martinoff family on 20 September, returning the next day. It was now time for the RAF Contingent to begin evacuating Medveja Gora and returning home. The following entries were made by Guy in his diary:

> 24th September: Allan and Boulmer left in afternoon. Livock and his party in the evening. This is the first lot of RAF to leave. Prasnik [Russian for party].
>
> 25th September: *Nairana* unit supposed to leave at 12o'clock. Put off till 6 pm. Finally left at midnight. 5 box trucks and Officers coach. Sleeping with Jimmy Noonan, Jinman and Isaac. Stephanov very upset at our leaving.

Stephanov was the Russian POW who Guy had put in charge of the other prisoners when working at the air station. With the prospect of being left as a prisoner of the Whites – and with the Reds presumably planning a new offensive, it's hardly surprising he was upset.

The last flight by a British officer from Medveja Gora took place as the unit was waiting to entrain. Captain Park flew a reconnaissance and bombing mission down the Lijma inlet with Lieutenant Matory, a Russian, as his observer. Enemy shipping was observed unloading what appeared to be massive reinforcements. A major Soviet offensive appeared imminent.

The trip back was not without incident. On arrival at Popoff on the 26th they discovered that *Nairana* had gone to Kandalaksha but would be back next day. Guy recorded the following comments:

27th September: Ship not in. Nobody seems to know anything. Had to turn out of our coach, spent most of the day moving our gear between Officer's Club and trains, which were supposed to go but didn't.

28th September: Went up to Kem at 12.30. Turned out of train. A general mess-up, got a box truck for the Officers. At 11.30 turned in.

29th September: Left for Kandalashka at 5 am. Prasnik all the way. Arrived at K at 9.30. Rawlinson's train there, also Bone, Dukes, Smithson. Our trucks moved onto pier in night.

30th September: Got our gear on two tugs and left for *Nairana* at 10 o'clock. Ship anchored 8 miles down gulf. Machines flying as there had been a Bolshy rising in the surrounding district.

The cause of all the delays and confusion was a rebellion by a group of 'Red Finns' who'd begun attacking trains and burning bridges. Livock's party had resorted to a show of force to get their train through Kandalashka 'fingering our revolvers like tough cine actors in a western in the face of a crowd of most unpleasant ruffians' (G Livock, *To the Ends of the Air* (HMSO, 1973; ISBN 0112901514)). Shortly afterwards a bridge north of the town was burned down, cutting off the *Nairana* unit who were due to be evacuated via Murmansk. Fortunately, *Nairana* was able to make her way by sea to pick them up and then moved to support a landing party that had been put ashore to suppress the rebels, but which had been badly cut up. One boat, with eleven members of the Highland Light Infantry aboard, was missing and intelligence suggested that some were being held prisoner. A show of force against the village of Kolvitza was decided upon, with Haines and Eades flying low over the village and a Monitor shelling the area. Their efforts were in vain, however, and it was left to the Whites to try and negotiate their release.

On 6 October *Nairana* reached Murmansk, spent a day taking on coal and sailed for Britain on the 8th. During their period in Russia her seaplanes had flown 616 hours of combat and communications missions, dropped 1,014 bombs with a combined weight of 28 tons,

321 gas bombs, 25,000 propaganda leaflets and fired 47,500 rounds of ammunition. Reconnaissance missions had photographed over 250 square miles. Working in close cooperation with the Lake Flotilla they sank, captured or severely damaged at least eight Soviet vessels and by persistent bombing of railways and bridges forced almost all enemy traffic to run at night. Isaac and Hayes both got the Distinguished Flying Cross for continuous good work and both Guy and Livock were mentioned in Daily Orders as being due to receive the Order of St Anne, 2nd Class, with crossed swords – a Russian medal. Unfortunately, the medals themselves never appeared.

Nairana put into the River Forth on 12 October. Following his return to Britain, Guy was posted briefly to HQ Coastal Area and was discharged from the RAF on 26 December 1919. He returned to Guernsey and was, for most of the rest of his long life, involved in farming and the breeding of Guernsey cattle. He married Nancy White, his lifelong companion, in 1926.

On the outbreak of the Second World War he voluntarily returned to the RAF as an administrative officer, being posted first to HQ No. 32 Balloon Barrage Group defending Portsmouth and then, on 18 May 1940, to HQ No. 50 (Training) Group at Reading, which controlled nine Elementary Flying Training Schools in the area as well as three Air Observer Navigation Schools and some supplementary flying instructors. He was appointed as a personnel officer and remained with the group throughout the war, rising to the rank of temporary squadron leader. His administrative duties took him on regular tours of the schools that came under group HQ and his attendance is noted at a number of administrative conferences.

The group ORB notes, in July 1943, 'Gardening is now carried out at all units in the Group, with the exception of Holwell Hyde. Six stations in the Group entered for the RAF Unit Garden Competition, and the gardens were judged by S/L B G Blampied (P2) of this Headquarters on 14th/15th July.' It is nice to see that Guy was able to continue his lifelong love of growing and gardening even during the war.

In 1944 Guy was presented with a Certificate of Good Service and attended a fortnight-long junior commanders' course. He was finally posted to No. 100 Personnel Despatch Centre for release from service on 20 October 1945.

Even though he was an administrative officer, he told me he was able to fly regularly, usually in Magister Trainers, as a way of ensuring he received flight pay.

Guy was closely involved for most of his life with the RNLI on Guernsey, where he was awarded the Institution's Gold Badge in 1972 and was elected an honorary life governor ten years later. He turned out to assist the lifeboatmen on almost every call that was made and would remain on station until the boat returned safely; in 1983 he wrote a book, *Mayday! Mayday!*, about the Guernsey lifeboat service.

Guy held numerous positions of authority on Guernsey including becoming a Jurat of the Royal Court, the highest honour bestowable by his fellow islanders. He was awarded the OBE in 1970.

Researching Guy Blampied

I first got in touch with Guy when I was researching Reggie Bone in the very early 1990s. In the hope of contacting people who'd served with him in his later career, I placed a short advert in one of the RAF magazines asking people to contact me. I received several replies from people who'd served with him in India in the 1920s and at Pembroke Dock in 1940 but I certainly wasn't expecting anything from his service in Russia in 1919. Over the course of a number of letters and phone calls we became quite friendly and he kindly sent me transcripts of his diary and some original, unpublished photographs. Having a diary to work with was invaluable, but there were a number of sources of material I used to check details and fill in the occasional gaps.

Guy's service record for the First World War period is in the AIR 76 series at TNA which is now available online via TNA's website in the Discovery section. In Guy's case, given that he served again in the Second World War, his record should, in theory, be retained by the Ministry of Defence but fortunately it is released. I had great pleasure in sending him a copy when the series was released in the early 1990s. The First World War record is in AIR 76/42 and can be searched for in TNA's website's Discovery section and downloaded (for a fee).

As he served in the RNAS prior to transferring to the RAF, Guy has a brief service record in ADM 273 series, in ADM 273/21 on p. 182. Though the record isn't online, the series is well indexed in TNA's catalogue.

Records for the RAF component of the North Russia Expeditionary Force are in AIR 1 series but you'll need to cast your search terms wide to find everything. Searching for '*Syren*' produces only 10 files, '*Murmansk*' 1 file, '*North Russia*' 22 and '*Nairana*' 7 files, some of which are references to the same file and some of which don't relate to the RAF Murmansk contingent – but it pays to make a varied and thorough search. Given that the RAF was part of a closely cooperating combined operation with the army and the navy it's also worth broadening your search into the WO and ADM series as well.

In 1973 Guy's colleague and commanding officer, Gerry Livock, who had had a distinguished RAF career, published his memoir *To the Ends of the Air*. This gives another perspective on the north Russia campaign and confirms some of the details in Guy's diary.

To trace Guy's RAF service in the Second World War I turned to four sources: the *London Gazette* online, which remains a useful source notwithstanding its known pitfalls, the *Royal Air Force List* and the *Royal Air Force Confidential List*, which is in AIR 10 series between AIR 10/3814 (April–May 1939) and AIR 10/5240 (October–December 1946). Unlike the public *RAF List*, which merely notes officer's seniority, the *Confidential List* does contain details of some postings, particularly of administrative officers, so by dipping into the range selectively I was able to build up a picture of where Guy was during the Second World War. The *Gazette* also records that on 1 January 1945 Guy was promoted to temporary squadron leader with back-dated seniority to 1 January 1944.

The ORB for 50 Group and its Appendices (in AIR 25/669 and AIR 25/670 respectively) provide the occasional vignette of his work.

A splendid obituary to a splendid gentleman appeared in the *Journal of the Royal Guernsey Agricultural Society* following Guy's death and, from this, much of the detail of his later career was obtained. It concluded: 'Guy Blampied is now resting from his many labours, but the good that he did during a remarkable life will be long remembered and his achievements treasured by those who now benefit from his foresight.' I was certainly both delighted and honoured to have worked with him in writing and researching the original article on which this chapter was based.

Chapter 4

ROYAL FLYING CORPS, AUXILIARY AIR FORCE AND SECOND WORLD WAR FLYING INSTRUCTOR – WILFRED BENNETT BEALE

Wilfred Bennett Beale epitomises a generation that fell in love with aviation during the First World War and continued to fly privately between the wars. His active service in the First World War was all too brief, being wounded in action within a couple of days of his arrival in the trenches, but after recovery (and a brief period when he did office work for MI5), like many other wounded officers, he transferred to the Royal Flying Corps and learnt to fly with 32 Training Wing, Middle East during 1918. Following the war, he pursued a career as a mining engineer in South Africa before returning to Britain to work in the family business, where he requalified as a pilot, was a private flying instructor and joined the Auxiliary Air Force, serving with 605 Squadron. Too old for combat flying when the Second World War broke out, he became a flying instructor, training the next generation of pilots at the Central Flying School at Upavon. Overworked and quite possibly stressed, he was killed, along with his pupil, in a flying accident in 1941.

Wilfred Beale, known to his friends as Tom, was born on 8 June 1898, son of Edgar Beale, a prosperous director of the Leicester Brewing and Malting Co. Ltd, and his wife, Edith, of Humberstone House, Humberstone, Leicestershire. He was educated at Oakham School, a private boarding school in Rutland, and later at

Eastbourne College where he was a member of the Officers' Training Corps (OTC). He left Eastbourne in May 1914 and it's not quite clear what he did next, but on 7 June 1916 he enlisted in the Inns of Court OTC, a Territorial Force unit that specialised in training young men who were hoping to get a commission. Here he received basic training in drill, musketry, entrenching and map reading and attended lectures and carried out field exercises. His time with the Eastbourne College OTC would no doubt have given him a lot of basic military training anyway. He was appointed to a commission with 3rd Battalion, The Buffs, on 1 September 1915. The 3rd Battalion were the old Militia (and now Reserve) Battalion for the regiment and he must have spent some months at the regimental depot in Canterbury before he was posted to serve with the 6th Battalion of the regiment.

Wilfred's time in the trenches was all too brief. He joined 6th Battalion on 15 March 1916, in the trenches at Vermelles, a village north-west of Loos and a couple of miles south of the La Bassée Canal. This was a coal-mining area and in keeping with this there was considerable mining activity at the front, with both sides tunnelling beneath their opponent's trenches to explode charges. A sufficiently strong charge could produce a sizeable crater with a lip several feet high overlooking the enemy trench. Craters like this in no-man's-land were heavily fought over as each side tried to gain a marginal advantage. On 17 March the Royal Engineers exploded a charge to try and collapse a German tunnel. The War Diary for the next day records,

> Officers from 7th Norfolk Regt arrived at 10.30 am to view trenches before taking over. Day quiet until 5.30 pm when the enemy opened very heavy fire with trench mortars on all the craters and with artillery on the back trenches. Garrisons of craters either killed or buried. At about 6.15 pm enemy blew a mine between CRATERS 1 & 2 on our side which completely filled in saps leading to craters and the top of SAVILLE ROW. At 6.30 pm bombardment lifted and enemy crept up to far lips of craters and proceeded to consolidate his position. B Coy moved forward to counter attack but could not advance across open owing to machine gun fire. Three Coys of West Kents sent up to reinforce, also some RE & Pioneers to dig out saps near lip of craters which we occupied – also to dig out WEST FACE.

Situation very quiet from 7 pm onwards. 2nd Lieuts Beale, Whitlock and Ruttle wounded & Lieutenant L E A Smith missing.

Lieutenant Beale was rapidly evacuated to Britain, where a medical board noted that he'd been wounded by fragments of a hand grenade penetrating the soft tissues of his thigh; two small fragments remained inside him. His wound was graded as slight and not permanent and he was incapacitated for military duty for two and a quarter months.

He was then graded as 'Fit for Home Service' and posted to the headquarters of MI5, the intelligence branch of the War Office which dealt with security and counter-espionage. His service with MI5, though ostensibly secret and 'glamorous', was in a purely administrative role in their H1 section, between December 1916 and April 1917. There was a Standing Order from the War Office that administrative posts, including intelligence, should be filled wherever possible by officers who had been wounded or were otherwise physically incapable of active service, thus freeing up active officers for service at the front. H1's duties were 'Compilation of historical records and statistics. Compilation, custody and issue of C.E. (Counter Espionage) Black Lists. Extracts from the press and distribution to the branches concerned. Compilation of summaries and précis of documents. Compilation and issue of records of important decisions. Compilation and issue of counter-espionage records from abroad. Printed Index and Lists of persons of interest to MI5.' Essentially, Tom was a glorified clerk – though one required to perform sensitive duties requiring intelligence, diligence and discretion.

Having returned to health, Tom was attached to 2nd Battalion the Leicestershire Regiment which was serving in Mesopotamia (now Iraq), but though the *War Office List* records this as from April 1917, he didn't actually join the battalion, which had seen considerable action in the meantime, until 19 November 1917. Presumably, in the meantime, he'd been on leave, possibly done some more training and then made his way to the Middle East, experiencing all those bureaucratic delays and confusions that accompany army life. For six weeks Tom got used to the new battalion, which was still receiving reinforcements and carrying out exercises and acting as a temporary source of labour, but then it was ordered to proceed by sea to Egypt and Palestine. The battalion embarked for Egypt on 1 January 1918 and made its way down the Tigris to Basrah, then on to Egypt, arriving on 22 January. Throughout February and March the battalion was engaged in a strenuous series of route marches and physical training exercises but on 31 March Tom was posted to the Yeomanry Base Depot at Kantara. At some point Tom seems to have decided that hanging about in depots and endless training was not sufficient. In June 1918 his RAF service record notes that he was now attached to the RAF at their Middle East Training Wing.

The training wing to which Tom was posted, No. 32 Training Wing, had been formed in November 1917 and consisted of No. 18 Training Depot Station at Ismailia, No. 20 Training Depot Station at Shallufa, No. 58 Training Squadron at Suez and No. 144 Training Squadron at Port Said.

The climate in Egypt was supposed to be better for the training of pilots and observers; certainly it allowed for training all-year round, though the heat of the day produced air currents that made flying for novices dangerous. One pilot who trained in Egypt at the end of 1917 recorded that work was suspended after the early morning until dusk and that,

> At this stage we were never in the air for more than half an hour, and as only one lesson a day was possible we pupils were left with much time on our hands. Between 11 am and about 4 pm we tried to sleep . . . for want of something to do I'm afraid we wasted many hundreds of hours playing poker.

Flying training had moved on quite a bit since Reggie Bone had first learnt to fly in 1913, though it had taken some time to do so. During the 1916 Battle of the Somme casualties among pilots new out to the front had been heavy and Major Robert Smith-Barry, CO of 60 Squadron had given much thought on how they should be trained initially. In December 1916 Smith-Barry was made Commander of 1 (Reserve) Squadron at Gosport and set about developing his theories.

The specialised Avro 504 biplane was used, with the trainee sitting in the front cockpit and the instructor sat in the back, with dual controls and a speaking tube through which he could pass the pupil his carefully prepared instructions (also known as 'patter'). Rather than avoid difficult and dangerous manoeuvres, the trainee was encouraged gradually to explore the aircraft's capabilities and taught how to put the aircraft into tricky situations such as spins and how to get out of them. With the aid of a carefully structured set of lectures the pupil was taught to explore the aircraft's capabilities fully and to be confident of his handling of it, whatever the circumstances.

Smith-Barry's methods (known as the Gosport or 'all in' method) were so successful that they were rapidly adopted by the RFC and the Egyptian flying schools also adopted them in 1917. Tom Beale learned to fly like this and the methods employed continued to be in use when he became a flying instructor himself later on.

Tom qualified as a pilot on 31 August 1918 (he is noted slightly later as being an SE 5 pilot, the SE 5 probably being the best single-seater fighter produced by Britain in the war) and was posted back to Britain on 15 October, though, of course, on his return, the Armistice had been signed and he was now surplus to requirements. After a brief period of sick leave he was transferred to the unemployed list on 6 March 1919.

Tom must have spent a period in South Africa, presumably working in the mining industry, as he's shown as returning to

Tom Beale (second left) with other officers of 605 Squadron in front of a Westland Wapiti at Castle Bromwich, 1932. (Courtesy of Ian Piper)

Britain on 25 June 1928 on the Union-Castle Line ship *Balmoral Castle*, landing at Southampton on that date, with his occupation given as mining engineer. He then changed direction and began working for the Leicester Brewing and Malting Co. Ltd, a small but prosperous and forward-thinking brewing company where his father was a director.

On 28 June 1931 Tom Beale passed his Royal Aero Club Aviator's Certificate for the second time, obtaining certificate number 9911. His index card shows that he was resident at Brook House, Rearsby, near Leicester; his occupation was still given as mining engineer and he passed his test in a Gipsy Moth DH 60 at Leicestershire Aero Club. He continued his connection with the club throughout the 1930s, serving on their committee in 1938 and acting as a flying instructor. In January 1932 he was appointed a flying officer with 605 (County of Warwick) AAF Squadron based at Castle Bromwich.

The Royal Auxiliary Air Force had been created in 1924 to help provide a reserve for the RAF; there was a certain social cachet attached to membership, with men generally being drawn from the middle and upper classes. 605 Squadron had been formed in 1926 at RAF Castle Bromwich as a bomber squadron and consisted entirely of volunteer pilots, supported by three Regular RAF officers, the Adjutant (administrative officer), an Assistant Adjutant and the Equipment Officer, with Regular ground crew and some NCO instructors. To all intents and purposes, the AAF was the RAF's equivalent of the Territorial Army, referring to the squadron HQ as a drill hall and to its weekend training sessions as camps; they also maintained close links to the County Territorial Association. By the time that Tom joined in 1932 they were flying the Westland Wapiti. As an AAF squadron, 605 members were expected to undertake regular weekend 'camps', on a paid and unpaid basis, evening work and an annual two-week camp on another airfield where they were treated as a Regular squadron.

The squadron already had a good reputation, having just won the Esher Trophy for the third time. Presented annually by Lord Esher, the trophy was competed for by AAF squadrons, with marks being awarded for bombing, formation flying, piloting ability and landings on a mark, gunnery, rigging, engine fitting, air photography and general squadron efficiency. Because it involved technical as well as flying tests it involved all ranks and helped to develop a squadron *esprit de corps*. 605 had won it for the first time of asking in 1927, again in 1930 and for the third time in 1931. Only a few weeks after Tom joined, on 25 February, Air Marshal HRH The Prince of Wales, who was making a visit to Castle Bromwich to attend the British Industries Fair there, presented the trophy personally.

Accompanied by Air Marshal Sir Geoffrey Salmond, Air Officer Commanding-in-Chief Air Defence of Great Britain, and Air Commodore W F MacNeece Foster, AOC No. 1 Air Defence Group, the Prince inspected a guard of honour from the squadron, noting that many of the men had First World War medals including a Military Medal and a Long Service and Good Conduct Medal. After saying that he'd visited the squadron before and enjoyed their hospitality he declared that it was a great achievement to have won the trophy three times, and twice in succession. He presented the trophy to Squadron Leader Wright, who called for three cheers, and the whole party adjourned to the drill hall.

Tom was a few years older than most of his brother officers, though a couple had also seen service in the First World War. Squadron Leader John Allan Cecil Wright, the squadron Commanding Officer (he'd formed the squadron in 1926), was born in 1886 and was commissioned into the Warwickshire Volunteers in 1905. When the Territorial Force was created in 1908 he set up a company of the Army Service Corps. He saw service with them in France and, as a major in the ASC, was attached to the RFC as a trainee observer in 1917. In the early 1930s he was chairman of Warne, Wright Rowland Ltd. Flying Officer Neville Nock had actually joined the RFC as a cadet on 29 August 1917, two days after his eighteenth birthday. After training in the Britain he had actually seen active service in France with 10 Squadron RAF in the last four months of the war and gone on to serve briefly with them in the Rhine Army. Transferred to the unemployed list in August 1919, he presumably spent the next four years qualifying as a dentist as he was described as a bank apprentice in 1917 but was later a dental surgeon. He rejoined the RAF as a Reserve officer in April 1923.

Flying Officer James Gummow, a printer, was born in 1905 and joined 605 Squadron in 1929. Flying Officer James Abell, born in 1909, was a solicitor's clerk. John Baker, born in 1907, was a law student when he joined the squadron in 1928. Flying Officer George Perry, a mining engineer, was born in 1905 and joined the squadron in 1927.

The squadron even had its own Victoria Cross – Flight Lieutenant

Cecil Leonard Knox, a Birmingham businessman, had won it in France as a Royal Engineer in 1918. His citation read:

On 22 March 1918 at Tugny, Aisne, France, Second Lieutenant Knox was entrusted with the demolition of 12 bridges. He successfully carried out this task, but in the case of one steel girder bridge the time fuse failed to act, and without hesitation he ran to the bridge under heavy fire, and when the enemy were actually on it, he tore away the time fuse and lit the instantaneous fuse, to do which he had to get under the bridge. As a practical civil engineer, Second Lieutenant Knox undoubtedly realised the grave risk he took in doing this.

Knox had learned to fly privately before joining the squadron but was later injured in a parachute accident and forced to give up flying.

The men of the squadron came from many backgrounds and *Flight* magazine noted that, 'those of them who were mechanics in civilian life usually preferred to do other duties. There were many men who were employed by Birmingham Corporation as well as shopmen and clerks in civilian life.'

The first recorded incident involving Tom Beale and the squadron was a bit embarrassing. Though details are sparse, his service record notes he was involved in an accident with AVRO J 8543 of 605 Squadron and Moth G-AA BH of the Midland Area Club at Castle Bromwich – '12.3.32. F/O W B Beale (uninjured)'. Presumably, this was a minor collision on the ground.

The squadron proceeded to Manston on 31 July 1932 for annual training. 'Following usual practice the Squadron operated as and performed the duties of a Regular Squadron. Tests in the Esher Trophy were judged by Flt Lieutenant Marsden A.D.G.B. Three days were spent at Eastchurch in the Bombing and Air Firing ranges and useful practice carried out by pilots and air gunners.' (squadron ORB).

The 1933 annual camp was also held at Manston and the ORB records that 21 officers and 132 airmen attended. In addition to working as a Regular squadron and being tested for the Esher Trophy, bombing and live-firing practice was carried out. What the ORB does not mention is that, in the course of live-firing exercises off the coast at Leysdown, an unfortunate accident resulted in the death of a young girl. *Flight* magazine recorded that,

Miss Jean Chesterton, aged 17, of Ilford, rowed out, with her younger sister, to retrieve a large ball drifting from the shore. While this boat was in the vicinity of a line of targets it was mistaken for a target by a gunner in the back seat of one of the machines who fired a burst at it. At the inquest the jury brought in a verdict of 'Death by Misadventure' which was the only verdict any sane jury could have returned. Various suggestions were put forward in an endeavour to prevent another such accident; no doubt the Air Ministry will do something in this direction. It does seem the two girls were a little unwise in rowing out in the direction of the target, especially as they had watched machines firing on those very targets many times previously. The parents are worthy of the sympathy of all, they have behaved magnificently throughout.

In fact, despite *Flight*'s account that the boat was 'in the vicinity' of the targets, most witnesses said that it was outside the target area. Squadron Leader Wright stated that he believed it was outside the area. The pilot, Flying Officer John Henry Wood, said during his evidence,

Just as I was getting on my course on the fifth circuit I heard what I took to be an early burst of firing. I glanced over my shoulder and noticed the direction in which Boahemia (the air gunner) was aiming and that he was not on target at all because I could actually see the targets come up under my wings. I was in a better position to see them than he was.

As well as the busy schedule of flying and training the squadron played sports regularly, with hockey matches against local teams recorded frequently, squash matches and the occasional mention of polo.

The nature of their day-to-day activities while at annual camp are explained nicely in the ORB for August 1934. The squadron flew to camp at Manston in formation, taking eleven Wapitis, two Avros and the Moth. The working routine adhered to was as in previous years, i.e., parade at hangars at 6am for daily instructions and 7.30–9am break for breakfast. After a parade at the huts the men were marched to the hangars for flying until ceasing work for the day at 12.45pm. Gun firing was carried out at Lydd ranges by all three flights.

Various tests for the Esher Trophy were also carried out. On 6 August the squadron was inspected by the Right Honourable Viscount Bearstead and by the Honourable Sir Philip Sassoon. Air Commodore Baldwin inspected the unit on 13 August and on the 18th there were swimming and polo matches between the officers and men; the officers won the swimming but lost the polo 4 goals to 1. On 19 August, 'The Squadron flew back to Castle Bromwich after a very successful camp; 22 officers and 151 airmen attended.'

In October 1934 the squadron received a Hawker Hart, the RAF's two-seater biplane light bomber which had entered service with the RAF generally in 1930. The ORB merely notes that on 27 October, 'The first Hart (K 3756) after being assembled at the unit was used for dual' (i.e., for dual instruction). On 19 November 1934 they received the good news that they had, once again, won the Esher Trophy. It was presented to them on 14 February 1935 by the Honourable Air Commodore Sir Philip Sassoon, the popular Under Secretary of State for Air, who, he reminded his audience, was also Honorary Air Commodore of 601 Squadron and, as such, he was 'filled with hatred and envy'. 'Alter the rules as we may,' he said, 'you still go on winning it.'

On 27 February 1936 the Esher Trophy was presented to the squadron for the sixth time. *Flight* magazine calling them 'that outstandingly efficient and enthusiastic unit'. Presentation of the trophy was by the Air Officer Commanding-in-Chief, Air Marshal Sir John Steel, KCB, KBE, CMG. The ceremony took place in the town hall, Birmingham and the chair was taken by the Lord Mayor, Alderman S J Grey JP. The presentation also marked the retirement from the squadron of Squadron Leader Wright, who was presented with a replica as a mark of thanks and respect for his ten years of dedication and hard work. In a short speech, Squadron Leader Wright spoke, as he put it, with mixed feelings, of the ten happiest years of his life and accepted the gift as acknowledgement of the work of everyone in the squadron. After the ceremony, the Lord Mayor and members of the Territorial Air Force Association entertained the squadron and their guests in the town hall.

Empire Air Day, 1936 was on Saturday 23 May and the ORB recorded,

Empire Air Day. The weather was very bad in the morning, but cleared up slightly in the afternoon, which resulted in rather a disappointing attendance, about 6,200. The following aircraft visited the station to take part in the flying programme:

1 Fury	
2 Bulldogs	CFS Upavon
1 Heyford	Boscombe Down
1 Sidestrand	Bicester

A Rota and an Avro Anson visited the station during the afternoon.

The AOC arrived by air and stayed for about 20 minutes. Owing to the weather the Secretary of State had to cancel his visit.

C Flight visited Desford, Braunstone, Anstey and Whitley during the afternoon.

On 19 July 1936 the squadron, consisting of nine Hart and three Avros, flew to Ratcliffe aerodrome, where they were entertained for lunch by Mr Lindsay Everard. A total of nineteen officers and five airmen attended. On the return journey the squadron landed at Braunstone, where they were given tea by the Leicester Aero Club. It seems a fair bet that Tom helped to arrange this!

The 1936 annual camp was held at RAF Aldegrove in Northern Ireland, the air party flying over with 12 Harts (including 1 Hart Trainer), 2 Avro Tutors and 1 Avro 504. The Avro was delayed at Carlisle for two days because it lacked the endurance to cross to Ireland against a strong crosswind. The ORB recorded, 'This camp was remarkable as being the first occasion on which the squadron attended armament training camp; it was the first occasion since its inception that it had been to camp anywhere except Manston, and also the first occasion on which Tutors were used for training instead of Avro 504's.'

By 1936 the RAF was in the process of expansion to meet the perceived threat from Hitler's Germany, and the Warwickshire Territorial Association volunteered to raise another Auxiliary squadron if requested. The ORB mentions an increasing number of new aircraft types visiting the station, a greater turnover of the squadron's Regular RAF officers, new equipment being used and there is generally a more serious tone to the squadron's activities –

61

though the regular round of social events such as dinner dances, luncheon parties, reunions and church parades continued.

The first use of a new bombing range allotted to the squadron took place in 1937, as well as the first use of wireless telegraphy equipment and the fitting and first use of oxygen equipment on its new Hawker Hinds. In a restructuring of Bomber Command 605 Squadron also became part of No. 2 Group, the squadrons of which were equipped with light and medium bombers.

Empire Air Day, 1937 was more successful than in the previous year, with double the public audience. The ORB noted,

> 29/05/1937: Empire Air Day. The weather was favourable and the attendance amounted to over 12,000. In addition a number of people burst through the barriers and large crowds were in the adjoining fields.
>
> A number of new aircraft visited the station including a Harrow, Blenheim, Anson and 3 Gladiators. A demonstration of these aircraft was carried out. A flight of the squadron visited Ratcliffe aerodrome during the afternoon. Cooperation during the last event of the programme – an attack on the aerodrome – was given by the 2nd Anti-Aircraft Machine Gun Battery, Royal Artillery, Lichfield.

In July 1937 a flight from the squadron overflew the Witney Aeronautical College garden party and then landed to display its Hawker Hinds to the crowds.

Summer camp was at Rochford in Essex in early August, though fog prevented there being as much use of the firing and bombing ranges as was usual. The squadron did take part in air exercises on 9 August with fair success. A total of 23 Auxiliary officers and 121 Auxiliary airmen participated in the camp, as well as the squadron's three Regular officers and 47 Regular airmen.

The threat of war really began to make itself felt during 1938, the year of the Munich Crisis, though in the early part of the year the ORB mainly refers to the usual round of dinners and entertainments.

In June 1938 the squadron made a formation flight during the inauguration of the new Wolverhampton Airport, in part to thank the Wolverhampton Flying Club for the fact that 75 per cent of their officers had first learnt to fly there. The summer camp that year took place at No. 6 Armament Training Station, Warmwell, Dorset. *Flight* magazine reported that bombing and firing practice took place over Chesil Bank with creditable scores being made, with formation flying exercises, photography, wireless and cross-country flying – and that proximity to the sea was an additional attraction for many of the men, for whom the camp was the equivalent of their annual holiday.

German pressure on Czechoslovakia to cede the Sudetenland during the summer of 1938 brought Britain and Germany to the verge of war. The squadron ORB records their part in the mobilisation of hundreds of Reserve airmen in anticipation of full-scale hostilities,

Emergency Mobilization during the Crisis of September October 1938

26/9/38	07.30 The Preparatory Order to Mobilize was received. This only applied to No 6 Mobilization Pool. The Preparatory Staff arrived between the hours 1600–2310 of this date.
27/9/38	1215 The Order to form Mobilization Pools was received and the necessary work was completed smoothly and rapidly. By 1500 hours the Pool was ready to receive Reservists and arrangements were completed to ration and house 1000 men. Fifteen hundred gas respirators were assembled in 131/2 hours, between 0950 and 2230 on 26th September 1938.
04/10/38	The Mobilization Pool was closed down this day
10/10/38	The Pool Administration Officer returned to his unit (Cranwell) at 1400 hours.

In October 1938 the squadron took part in a joint exercise with the British Thomson-Houston works at Rugby with the squadron staging a mock bombing attack for the benefit of training the works Air Raid Precaution staff.

With the approach of war Tom relinquished his commission with 605 Squadron AAF on 10 January 1939 and was appointed to the *RAF General List* with rank of flight lieutenant. At the age of 40 he was probably too old for combat flying, but as a qualified flying instructor there was plenty for him to do. In June 1939, presumably after a refresher course in flying instruction, he became fully qualified and on 23 August 1940 he was posted to the Central Flying School at Upavon, as an instructor in the flying squadron.

An Air Ministry pamphlet, *Hints on Flying Instruction*, published in March 1941 gives some idea of the non-technical aspects of the art of instruction,

> When the Flying Instructor had been taught to fly accurately and to demonstrate his actions with synchronised 'patter', only the foundation of his profession has been provided for him. The most skilful pilot with the most perfect patter can still make a bad instructor, and the average pilot with good average patter can make an excellent instructor. The difference being that the one almost disregards the characteristics and foibles of his different pupils, while the other makes a constant study of his pupils in order that he may get the very best out of them.
>
> If you are slack in manner and appearance then you will inevitably breed a race of pilots, all your own, which tends to be slack in manner and appearance. Although you may not realise it, everything you do and say is mentally noted by your pupils, on duty and off duty. Your appearance in uniform should be good. Nobody should be able to teach you anything about punctuality. Move about as though you have a definite purpose in life. Don't run down ground training. Some of it is admittedly dull, and lots of it may seem to you to smack of the kindergarten. Those in authority have good reason to believe that it has high value however, so support their authority and don't undermine it. Don't criticise superiors. Don't discuss your own pupils, or other instructors or superior officers, with pupils. Along with priests and physicians you share a lot of confidences. Respect them.

Pressure was always on to train and turn out newly qualified pilots; in February 1941 a conference of 23 (Training) Group at Upavon commented upon the shortage of experienced flying instructors. Many experienced flight commanders had been sent out to flying schools in the Dominions. Senior flying instructors (those with over six months' training experience) were doing two-year tours of duty and this was felt to be too long. As a flight commander and experienced instructor, Tom would have had the number of pupils training under him at any one time reduced from six to four and though he was promoted to Deputy Chief Flying Instructor, which cut down on his actual instruction in the air, it did mean extra work supervising the other instructors. The pressure was unrelenting.

On 6 June 1941 Tom was recommended for the award of the Air Force Cross. His commendation for the medal reads,

> As a Flight Commander and recently as Deputy Chief Flying Instructor of Central Flying School this Officer has performed work of outstanding merit.
>
> He has completed 1000 hours of instructional flying since June 1939 and during the past twelve months has done 600 hours giving instruction and testing pilots. He has been at C.F.S. since August 1940, and despite his age (42) he has not spared himself and has shown marked energy and devotion to duty, setting a fine example to those who work under him.

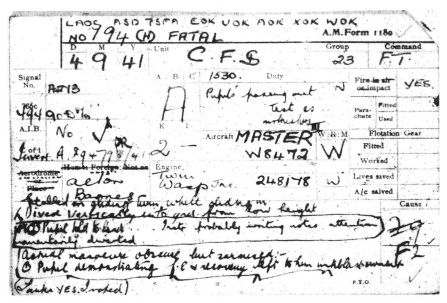

Tom Beale's Accident Card describing the fatal accident at Alton Barnes. (Courtesy of the RAF Museum)

Tom was never to receive the medal personally. He was killed in an air crash in September.

The CFS ORB is terse, the sole entry, dated 4 September 1941, reads,

> S/LDR BEALE and P/O Brown killed in flying accident at Alton Barnes Relief Landing Ground.

Next day it records,

> INQUEST on S/Ldr Beale and P/O Brown was held in school-room at 1600 hours. A verdict of accidental death was returned.

On 6 September it notes,

> INVESTIGATION by W/Cdr Whitelock into crash of Master 8472 and deaths of S/Ldr Beale and P/O Brown.

The result of the investigation is recorded briefly on the accident record card held by the RAF Museum at Hendon. It was Pilot Officer Brown's passing out test as an instructor and the aircraft stalled while in a gliding turn while gliding in; the aircraft dived vertically into the ground from a low height. Though the accident was unobserved, it was surmised that the pupil was demonstrating a forced landing, had been told to lead, and that Tom Beale was probably writing notes and his attention was momentarily diverted.

Tom's death certificate gives the cause of death as 'Multiple injuries sustained when aeroplane in which he was flying was crashed from causes unknown.' The AFC was awarded posthumously.

Wilfred 'Tom' Beale is buried in Upavon Cemetery in Wiltshire in Row D, Grave 6. The inscription reads 'His sun went down while it was yet day'. He was 42. Pilot Officer George Henry Brown, who was killed with him, is buried alongside in Grave 5.

Researching Wilfred Beale

Records of Wilfred Beale's military career begin with his First World War army officer's file, WO 339/39704. It contains some details of his army career including his initial attestation papers showing he enlisted first in the Territorial Force (predecessors of the Territorial Army) for the Inns of Court OTC, with the obvious intention of becoming an officer immediately. Much of the rest of his file consists of medical sheets detailing the wounds he suffered in France from the medical boards he attended.

The War Diary for 6th Battalion the Buffs is in WO 95/1860 and this is one of the First World War War Diaries available to be downloaded from TNA's website for a very reasonable price. The War Diary for 2nd Battalion, Leicestershire Regiment is in WO 95/4715; though at time of writing this is not available online, it is one of the War Diaries that will be going online in due course.

There is little on Tom's MI5 service. KV 1/59, a list of MI5 staff up to 31 December 1919, basically just confirms the dates of his service and the regiment he was serving with at the time. A further sub-list in KV 1/52 gives snapshots of MI5 section staff and confirms Tom's service with H1.

Details of his initial service with the RFC and RAF are in AIR 76/29, which are available through the Discovery section of TNA's website. The record gives details of his service in the Middle East and, though records are supposed to cease in 1920, of his service with 605 Squadron AAF between 1934 and 1939. Details of the other 605 Squadron officers referred to in this chapter are also available in AIR 76.

When it comes to his training period in Egypt, as is so often the case when looking at RFC and RFC training squadrons, few records survive. There seems to have been a general destruction of day-to-day records once the Official History of the War in the Air was completed. It is possible to make some general observations on the subject based on general files of correspondence and histories, notably AIR 1/408/15/240/2 – 'RAF: History of Training in Egypt, 1916–1918'; AIR 1/678/21/13/2085 – 'Notes on Training, Egypt'; AIR 1/2054/204/409/12 – '32 Training Wing'.

Though the actual paperwork for the investigation into Tom's final crash does not appear to survive, the accident record card is held on microfilm at the RAF Museum at Hendon and provides basic details. The museum kindly sent me a copy. Please note that there are no indexes that refer to crew members, aircraft type or location of the accident – to request a copy you will need to know the aircraft type and date of the accident.

As ever, the *Flight* magazine archive at http://www.flight-

Tom Beale's grave at Upavon Cemetery, where he lies surrounded by colleagues from both wars. (Author's Collection)

global.com/pdfarchive/index.html proved invaluable in locating stories about 605 Squadron in the 1930s, occasionally providing those little personal stories that the official documents fail to capture.

The ORB for 605 Squadron between 1926 and December 1939 is in AIR 27/2087. In common with the other squadron ORBs, it's now online in the Discovery section on TNA's website.

There's a useful website devoted to 605 Squadron at http://www.605squadron.co.uk/Home.htm, which gives some basic details of its history, bases, commanding officers, casualties and honours and awards.

Chapter 5

BATTLE OF BRITAIN PILOT – GUY MARSLAND

B orn on 5 November 1919, Guy Marsland joined the RAF on a short service commission in April 1939. After completing his flying training he joined 245 Squadron at Leconfield in early November 1939. Posted to 253 Squadron at Kenley on 24 September 1940, he damaged a Bf 109 fighter on 7 October, claimed a Bf 109 destroyed on 29 October and shared a Dornier 17 bomber on 22 November. Later in the war he served in the Far East and after the war held a number of administrative posts. Retiring from the RAF on 1 October 1958 as a squadron leader, he retained the rank of wing commander. He later became a successful antiques dealer and died in 1983.

Guy joined the RAF on a short service commission on 15 April 1939. This type of commission, introduced by Hugh Trenchard in the early 1920s, was designed to produce a generation of young pilots who would serve for a few years and then transfer to the RAF Reserve and wouldn't clog up the RAF as ageing officers at a later date. By 1939 the terms were to serve for four years on the active list followed by two years in the Reserve. Having been commissioned as an acting pilot officer, he was sent to learn to fly at the civil flying school at Redhill, where he was taught the basics. In April 1939 he was posted to No. 6 Flying Training School at Little Rissington, as part of 12 Course, consisting of forty-one officers and eight airmen pupils, to learn service flying. Having passed through the school, he was appointed a probationary flying officer and posted to 245 Squadron, which was forming at RAF Leconfield in East Yorkshire, to fly twin-engine Blenheim fighters. On arriving at the squadron, along with thirteen other newly qualified pilot officers, there were only three Magister aircraft for training purposes. Some Blenheims did arrive, but it was already decided that the squadron were to be re-equipped with single-seater Hurricane fighters and in January 1940 some Fairey Battle aircraft arrived so the pilots could learn to fly single-seaters. The first three Hurricanes arrived at the end of January but were short of spares so that training didn't really commence until a further nine were delivered by ferry pilots on 15 March. The squadron ORB noted, 'It is a grand sight and the obvious pleasure to the pilots and airmen is very heartening. We have done the "per ardua" part, which can be freely translated in our case to mean marking time. Now for the stars.'

Full-scale training now followed so that by the first week in April nearly all the pilots were trained in battle climbs and fighter attacks, in the use of the radio telephone and were being trained in working in coordination with the Sector Controller. By the 23rd the squadron was ready enough to launch its first real scramble, though the flight that took off was recalled almost immediately. On 30 April aircraft from the squadron were again scrambled and this time flew 90 miles out over the North Sea without seeing their quarry.

On 12 May the squadron was moved to RAF Drem near Edinburgh, but events in France (where the German invasion of Belgium and France began on 10 May) began to influence events. A Flight was sent to France on the 16th and on the 28th fifteen aircraft of the squadron (including Guy) flew south to RAF Hawinge in Kent. On 30 May Guy took part in a patrol over Dunkirk but due to bad visibility the patrol became separated and Guy was one of four pilots who made a forced landing near Southend due to lack of fuel; his aircraft was rendered unserviceable. On 1 and 2 June he took part in composite formations protecting shipping over Dunkirk, the final stages of the evacuation. On 10 June he was one of nine Hurricanes who escorted thirty-three Blenheims on a bombing raid over Rouen and over the next three days took part in offensive patrols along the French coast trying, but failing, to draw the Luftwaffe into battle. On the 14th Guy was pilot of one of eleven aircraft that accompanied a bombing raid to Bethune which was accomplished without incident, though there was heavy anti-aircraft fire that damaged one Hurricane. Other patrols followed over southern England and northern France, including one over the French coast in the vicinity of Dieppe in which German aircraft were seen on the ground, but none were encountered in the air.

On 30 June 245 Squadron flew north to RAF Turnhouse near

Edinburgh from where they flew sector patrols and provided air escorts to convoys along the Scottish coast, again without encountering the enemy. On 20 July they were ordered to RAF Aldegrove in Northern Ireland and eighteen Hurricanes flew across in the afternoon followed by essential ground staff, who flew across in three transport aircraft slightly later. From Aldegrove they again flew sector patrols, scrambled occasionally when enemy aircraft were suspected to be approaching and flew air cover for convoys. On 24 September Guy Marsland was posted back to the mainland to serve with 253 Squadron at RAF Kenley.

By this time Guy was an experienced pilot with many hours of flying time under his belt and plenty of operational flying, though he'd yet to make contact with the enemy. With 253 flying regular scrambles and patrols against German intruders, it was only a matter of time.

The Battle of Britain had now reached what, in retrospect, was its final phase. Heavy losses to their bomber formations had caused the Germans to switch mainly to night bombing. However, during the day German fighters, mostly Me 109s but occasionally Me 110s, were sent over carrying bombs in small and large-scale nuisance raids aimed at engaging the RAF fighters and disrupting defensive operations over the South East. Coming in high and fast, the raiders gave little warning, even to radar so the RAF had to use regular patrols between 15,000 and 20,000ft, directed onto the intruders once the radar picked them up.

On 7 October Guy was on patrol over Hawkinge, lost contact with

Hurricane IIbs of 253 Squadron being worked on by ground crew. (Author's Collection)

the remainder of the patrol and met a formation of enemy fighters that had been operating briefly over London. The RAF website devoted to the Battle of Britain describes the raid as, 'At 1630 hours a further flight of 30 enemy aircraft crossed the coast at Dungeness, penetrated to Central and North East London, but quickly turned back to France at 1645 hours.' Guided by anti-aircraft fire, Guy found the Me 109s in the vicinity of Biggin Hill and his combat report describes the action,

> I was Green 2 of the squadron formation flying at 24,000 feet above Hawkinge. I saw Yellow 2 break formation. I watched him going down. At the same time I saw one unidentified aircraft following him. I covered him and the aircraft turned away. I could not find my own formation again, so I patrolled south of Biggin Hill at 23,000 feet. Twenty ME 109's were observed coming from the direction of London. I delivered a beam attack on a section of three firing a 8–9 burst and saw several small pieces break off from one aircraft. I broke away without observing any other result and returned to base where I discovered that Yellow 2 had broken formation due to engine trouble.

Small-scale raids designed to test the defences and tire pilots to prevent them attempting to attack the main night attacks continued for the next three weeks with 253 Squadron flying their usual patrols attempting to intercept them.

On 29 October Guy was on patrol with B Flight, 253 Squadron when they encountered 16 Me 110s and Me 109s over the Surrey/Sussex border. His report says,

> I was Green 1 weaving for 253 Squadron at 20,000 feet. I broke away to engage enemy aircraft. I followed one aircraft down to 3,000 feet but was not able to open fire. I positioned myself at Gatwick. At 1700 hours I sighted one ME 109 at 4,000 feet travelling south. I climbed up to line astern and opened fire at 150 yards. Tracer passed over and under main planes of E/A. The 109 half rolled. I last saw him about 300 feet from the ground in the vicinity of Horsham. The 109 was on his side and I consider about to crash. Horsham Observer Corps report one ME 109 crashed at 1706.

The local newspaper, the *West Sussex Times*, reported the incident,

A Messerschmidt single-seat fighter 'plane was shot down at Plummers Plain on Tuesday evening, after machine-gunning a party of farm labourers in the field below. A Spitfire [*sic*] put only one burst of fire into the German 'plane and it crashed along the field, dragging hurdles with it. The pilot, his clothes on fire, was pulled out from the blazing 'plane by several civilians and a member of the Military Police, who burned his hands badly effecting the rescue.

The pilot, the holder of the Iron Cross, was taken by an ambulance to hospital after his boots and clothes had been cut from him. He was unconscious, and died later. Pieces of wreckage, together with the pilot's gear and clothing, were strewn about the field, while the body of the machine blazed furiously, magnesium flares sending up a blue flame. Before dusk men were on the scene and got the fire under control with buckets of water and stirrup pumps.

The pilot, Alfred Lenz, died later of burns in Horsham Hospital and now lies in grave 27, block 1, row 1 at Cannock Chase.

The Battle of Britain was now officially over, but nuisance raids by the Luftwaffe continued, as did the regular patrols by 253 squadron. On 22 November a patrol of three aircraft from A Flight encountered two Dornier 17 light bombers over the Sussex coast. Guy's report says,

Red section 253 Squadron took off at 1145 hours on sector reconnaissance. When at 10,000 feet near Beachy Head Red 1 was advised that one E/A was approaching Dungeness at 3,000 feet. Section patrolled Beachy Head Dungeness and observed one D.O. 17 Z flying north in and out of cloud at 3,000 feet, section attacked in rotation from out of the sun and E/A was seen to dive vertically into the ground three miles north of Newhaven.

Red Section was continuing a sector reconnaissance near Beachy Head after previous combat when one D.O. 17 was sighted 8 miles south of Beachy Head flying west. Section attacked in rotation from astern and E/A turned south. Section expended all ammunition remaining over from previous combat and silenced both E/A's rear gunners and port starboard engine out of action.

A further report from 11 Group Fighter Command of the same date records,

Combat took place near Newhaven at 1220 hours on 22/11/40. Three Hurricanes Red Section 253 Squadron led by F/Lt Duke-Woolley left Kenley at 11.53 hours on a sector reconnaissance and proceeded to Beachy Head at 10,000 feet. Red Section who were flying in a loose line astern, upon being advised that one enemy aircraft was approaching from the south east at 3,000 feet, reduced height to 8,000 feet and sighted a D.O. 17 Z flying in and out of cloud at 3,000 feet Red Section dived and attacked individually from the rear, Red 1 giving E/A 3 bursts of 4 seconds, Red 2 two attacks from astern and one from port beam, Red 3 one attack of 4 seconds from starboard beam. The E/A port engine caught fire after which E/A dived vertically into the ground between Brighton and Lewes. There was a terrific explosion and the wreckage was strewn over a wide area. Two bodies were found, one with the Iron Cross. The E/A's bomb load exploded some 45 minutes after it crashed. Red section continued the reconnaissance and a second DO 17 Z was sighted 6 miles south east of Beachy Head at 4,000 feet. Section dived from 12,000 feet and again attacked individually from astern. The E/A was last seen 3 miles off the French coast with starboard engine out of action and rear gunners had ceased firing. Red section returned to base. Three Hurricanes landed Kenley 1340 hours.
    Weather 10/10ths cumulus cloud, 1,000–3,000 feet; 2/10ths stratus cloud 4,000–5,000 feet. Visibility above clouds excellent.
    Both E/A shared between   Red 1 F/Lt Duke Woolley
                                   Red 2 F/O Eckford
                                   Red 3 P/O Marsland

On 24 March 1941 Guy was posted to 232 Squadron, flying Hurricanes out of RAF Elgin to cover shipping and protect against opportunist Luftwaffe raids. This was a posting of just a few weeks before he was sent to 56 Operational Training Unit at RAF Sutton Bridge in Lincolnshire, which trained new pilots to fly the

18.2.42	As weather was not too good in the morning, there was very little flying. Red section patrolled Yarmouth and Lowestoft in the afternoon and there were three Scrambles. Air firing and practice cine gun were also carried out. F/L Marsland was posted to R.A.F. Coltishall w.e.f. 17/2/42 pending posting overseas. P/O De Houx and F/Sgt Mercer ordered to report to Admiralty.

Extract from 137 Squadron ORB showing Guy Marsland being posted away from the squadron on 18 February 1942. (TNA AIR 27/954)

Hurricane. As an experienced Hurricane pilot, he was no doubt in great demand as an instructor and stayed with the unit for over six months.

On 15 December 1941 Guy was posted to 137 Squadron, flying twin-engined Whirlwind fighters over the southern North Sea from RAF Matlaske, a satellite station to RAF Coltishall in Norfolk. With four 20mm cannon mounted in the nose, the Whirlwind was not, in itself, a bad aircraft. However, there were problems with its engines and by the time it came into service it was already somewhat out of date, having been intended as an escort fighter for Bomber Command, which was already switching to night operations, for which the Whirlwind was not equipped.

In his brief time with 137 Squadron, after a period learning the new machine, Guy flew a few scrambles against what were thought to be German raiders, though without making contact. On Christmas Day 1941 he flew escort duty for a Lysander searching for a reported dinghy seen about 50 miles off the coast, but nothing was found. He was lucky not to have been sent on a patrol on 12 February 1941 when squadron aircraft on routine patrol ran into a huge Luftwaffe formation covering the break out into the Atlantic of the *Scharnhorst* and *Gneisenau*, and four aircraft were lost.

On 18 February 1942 the squadron ORB records, 'F/L Marsland posted to RAF Coltishall w.e.f. 17/2/42 pending posting overseas.' Though his service record makes no mention of the fact, Guy was posted to 136 Squadron in the Far East. Equipped with Hurricanes, it had been sent to India in November 1941 but its destination had been changed to Burma following the Japanese invasion. In his book *Take Mary to the Pictures – A Fighter Pilot in Burma 1941–1945*, Alan Kitley, a 136 Squadron pilot, says that their Hurricanes were clapped-out Mark I aircraft, probably ones that had been used previously for training. Presumably, Guy was flown to the Far East, though it's unclear when he arrived – a retrospective note in 136

75

DATE OF EFFECT	P/A	UNIT	GRP.	CMD.	H/O
6. 2. 39		Civil Flg. Sch. Redhill			
15. 4. 39	P	1 Depot.	24 T		H
29. 4. 39	P	6 Flg. Trg. Sch.	23 T		H
6. 11. 39	P	245 Sqn.			H
24. 9. 40	P	253 Sqn.			H
24. 3. 41	P	232 Sqn.			H
6. 5. 41	P	56 Op. Trg. U.			H
15. 12. 41	P	137 Sqn.		FC	H
18. 2. 42	—	137 Sqn.		FC	H
5. 12. 42	P	224 Group		India	O
10. 6. 43	P	169 Wing		India	O
30. 11. 43	P	H.Q. Spec. Force		ACSEA	O
20. 3. 44	P	189 Wing		ACSEA	O
3. 9. 44	P	168 Wing (now 903 Wing)		ACSEA	O
1. 10. 44	P	Wing H.Q. Patel		ACSEA	O
18. 4. 45	P	908 Wing		ACSEA	O
1. 10. 45	P	Air H.Q. French Indo-China		ACSEA	O
19. 1. 46	P	1 Personnel Desp. Centre	28	TTC	H
18. 3. 46	P	11 Recruit Centre	22	TTC	H
24. 5. 46	P	4 Recruit Centre	22	TTC	H
5. 6. 46	P	Empire Radio Sch. Debden	24	TTC	H
14. 3. 47	—	Empire Radio Sch.	24	TTC	H
30. 3. 48	A	RAF Component, Visual Inter-Services Trg.			H
10. 4. 48		&Research Estab. Erlestoke Camp.			
14. 10. 48	P	5 Personnel Desp. Centre	28	TTC	H
26. 10. 48	P	RAF. Del. Greece. A.M./Spl. Duty List/Misc/445		AM	O
8. 11. 49	P	Air Ministry U.	28	TTC	H
20. 12. 49	P	Flg. Refresh. Sch. Finningley	21	FTC	H
8. 2. 50	P	Duxford	11	FC	H
20. 3. 50	A	Off. Adv. Trg. Sch. Bircham Newton	22	TTC	H
16. 5. 50					

P = POSTING
A = ATTACHMENT

(4) MOV

(MOVEMENTS CONTINUED OVERLEAF)

NAME

MARSLAND   GUY

Guy Marsland's service record erroneously showing him continuing to serve with 137 Squadron when he was actually with 136 Squadron in Burma and India. (Author's Collection)

Squadron ORB says that he was posted to them with effect from 19 February 1942 as a flight commander but he can't have arrived on that date. During the retreat from Burma, which the squadron was covering in its dilapidated Hurricanes, record keeping became problematic. Certainly, he was with them in the third week in March. Alan Kitley recorded:

The blitz came on the 23rd and 24th March. On both these days Akyab and the docks were attacked by large formations of Japanese bombers with fighter escorts . . . I am talking about a maximum of roughly fifteen–twenty clapped out Hurricanes attempting to attack waves of bombers being protected by formations of some twenty, thirty, who knows – Japanese fighters. They covered the sky like swarms of mosquitoes. In the ensuing one-sided battles we claimed some ten kills and many probables. But in effect we were shot out of the air and it was a miracle that of the several Hurricanes shot down, all but one of our pilots survived having either baled out or force landed.

Among the claims was one for Guy Marsland, who claimed to have shot down a Nakajima Ki 43 fighter on 23 March.

With their effective aircraft reduced to just five Hurricanes, the squadron was evacuated to India. Alan Kitley was one of the few pilots who was able to nurse his aircraft to Chittagong and then on to Dum Dum airfield at Calcutta. Guy and the remainder of the squadron were evacuated by sea.

Reunited at Alipore, the squadron was based at an airfield used by the Bengal Flying Club and Guy was made Flight Commander of B Flight. Alan Kitley explained the squadron organisation nicely when he wrote,

Typically a fighter squadron was commanded by a Squadron Leader and had eighteen aircraft, approximately thirty–thirty five pilots, two hundred ground personnel to service the aircraft [etc.] . . . the operational structure was centred on two flights, A & B, each commanded by a flight lieutenant. Each Flight had nine aircraft, some fifteen pilots and first line servicing crews headed by a flight sergeant.

In addition, there was an adjutant who helped the squadron leader with administration, an engineering officer, a medical officer and an intelligence officer. The whole squadron would number between 200 and 300 of all ranks. Loyalty to the squadron was strong but loyalty to the individual flight could be stronger. Alan Kitley explained, 'Until I became a Squadron Commander I made sure that regardless of what squadron I was in, I was in the B Flight; to me B Flight were action men and A Flight were poofs.'

For some ten weeks between 26 June and 5 September 136 Squadron operated from one of the more unusual airfields ever used by the RAF – the Red Road, one of the main thoroughfares in the very centre of Calcutta, described by Alan Kitley as 'the equivalent of The Mall'. The Red Road was wide enough to land a Hurricane on, with grass strips on either side, but the camber of the road made it essential that pilots landed dead centre to avoid the aircraft automatically swerving off the road and colliding with a low wall. In addition, a statue of Queen Victoria at one end of the road provided an interesting challenge when landing or taking off!

The squadron provided air defence of the Calcutta area from March 1942, though the Japanese Army and air force had exhausted themselves during their advance through Burma and real air raids were few. Unfortunately, as there was no radar and few other means of identifying aircraft there were frequent 'scrambles' against what turned out to be friendly aircraft. As flight commander Guy seems to have taken part in only a few of these sorties but the squadron ORB does list him flying operationally either as a 'scramble' in response to air-raid sirens or on convoy patrols, covering shipping movements in the Bay of Bengal.

On 5 December 1942 Guy was posted to 224 Group to fill the squadron leader ops vacancy. Thereafter, since he no longer flew operationally (though he did still fly) his movements and postings become harder to trace. Various orders published in the Group ORB Appendices tell some kind of a story:

30/12/1942	Reposted HQ 224 Group as supernumary.
15/12/1942	Authorised to be accommodated in the Officer's Mess w.e.f. 05/12/1942 and draw appropriate allowances.
24/12/1942	Departed Chittagong 0900 hours.
24/12/1942	Arrived Calcutta 1200 hours by air.
27/12/1942	Departed Calcutta 0500 hours.
28/12/1942	Arrived Chittagong 1000 hours by rail. Ops Duties.
24/01/1943	Detached from this unit and attached to HQ 165 Wing for Special Duties.
03/02/1943	Transferred to the RAFO on completion of the active service period of his Short Service Commission. To be treated as

	w.e.f. date of transfer as an officer of the reserve called for Air Force Service and to take command precedence as at present.
05/02/1943	Re-posted to this unit w.e.f. 05/02/43 to fill Squadron Leader Ops vacancy.
18/02/1943	Detached from this unit and Attached as RAF Liaison Officer, 14th Division.
08/05/1943	Ceased to be attached to HQ 14 Division on return to this unit.
08/05/1943	Detached from this unit and attached to 169 Wing.
22/05/1943	Ceased to be attached 169 Wing on return to this unit.
23/05/1943	Arrived in Calcutta from 169 Wing (While in Calcutta in hospital from 24/05/43 to 01/06/1943).
01/06/1943	Discharged from No 47 BGH Calcutta.
08/06/1943	Departed Calcutta; arrived 224 Group Chittagong by air.
10/06/1943	Posted from this unit to No 169 Wing for Squadron Leader Flying Post.

With his undoubted experience and, presumably, considerable administrative ability, Guy seems to have become one of those 'backroom boys' whose hard work in organising, planning and coordinating air operations was invaluable at a time when the RAF in India was reorganising but at the same time flying and fighting over Burma against a Japanese foe that proved resilient and capable. 224 Group's ORB for 1943 show that the group was flying offensive patrols over enemy lines, defending against Japanese raids over their own territory and attacking ground and coastal targets

41940 F/Lt G.Marsland (A/S/Ldr)   G.D   Arrived in Calcutta from No 169 Wing 23.5.43 (Whilst in Calcutta in Hospital from 24.5.43. to 1.6.43. See entry in this P.O.R. and in P.O.R. No 40/43) Departed Calcutta 8.6.43. Arrived No 224 Group Chittagong 8.6.43. by Air. (See entry under "B" Attachments in this P.O.R.) Authy:- H.Q. No 224 Group.

Excerpt from 224 Group Orders showing some of Guy Marsland's movements in 1943. (TNA AIR 25/944)

throughout the year. In November 1943 Guy was appointed to HQ of Special Force, the 'Chindits', who operated deep behind enemy lines and were supplied by air. In March 1944 Guy was posted to 189 Wing as Squadron Leader, Flying Ops and on 6 June to 168 Wing as officer in charge of flying. In August he supervised the training of Thunderbolt squadrons, preparatory to the squadrons joining the wing. On 1 October 1944 he was posted to Wing HQ, then to 908 Wing HQ where he was still serving on VJ Day.

Guy returned to Britain in 1946 and continued to serve until 1958 in a series of mainly administrative posts. He spent a year at the Empire Radio School at RAF Debden in Essex, time as part of the RAF Component of the Visual Inter-Services Training and Research Establishment at Erlestoke Camp near Devizes which specialised in deception and camouflage and was then, in October 1948, posted to the RAF Delegation to Greece. Here the RAF was giving technical and administrative assistance to the Royal Hellenic Air Force which was engaged in fighting insurgents during the Greek Civil War. Originally paid for by Britain, immediately after the Second World War, the RHAF was equipped mainly with British aircraft, though by the time Guy was posted there most of the funding was from the Americans who had become responsible for advising the Greeks on operations. The British Mission mainly gave technical advice and training. Though the mentions of Guy in the surviving paperwork are few, it seems likely he was one of the squadron leaders posted to the advanced airfields and he may have flown occasionally.

Returning to Britain in November 1949, Guy held various posts with Fighter Command and Technical Training Command, then spent eighteen months with Coastal Command at RAF Calshot between March 1952 and October 1953. He was at the Aircrew Selection Centre at Hornchurch from 1954 to 1957 and his final posting in 1957 was to the Air Ministry, where he served in the department of the Director General, Manning. He retired on 1 October 1958.

Researching Guy Marsland – Another Error in a Service Record

It's curious sometimes how things turn up. I had been looking for a previously unresearched Battle of Britain pilot and was chatting with my Dad when he happened to mention that he thought one of his old geography teachers, 'Kiki' Marsland, had been a Second World War fighter pilot – and that he'd seen what he thought was his name mentioned on the Battle of Britain Memorial at Capel le Ferne in Kent. Subsequent research has shown that my Dad's teacher is not the same man, but by this time I had the bit between my teeth and decided to press on and find out more about a man who had continued to serve through the 1950s, in the period when the RAF moved into the jet age and the atomic bomb. I never did find out the truth about my father's teacher!

Getting started was very easy. The Battle of Britain has been a popular subject for research for many years and, though I'm always cautious about online sources, the first port of call had to be Google. Thankfully, Marsland is not a particularly common name so I simply typed in Marsland Battle of Britain and received confirmation of his existence. The RAF Battle of Britain Roll of Honour at http://www.raf.mod.uk/history/BattleofBritainRollofHonour.cfm confirmed that Pilot Officer G Marsland flew with 245 and 253 Squadrons and a list of RAF Aircrew in the Battle of Britain on Wikipedia at http://en.wikipedia.org/wiki/List_of_RAF_aircrew _in_the_Battle_of_Britain named him as Guy Marsland, stating that he was Pilot Officer Guy Marsland of 245 and 253 Squadrons and suggested that he died in 1983.

An item on the BBC WW2 People's War website suggested that Guy Marsland had later flown with 136 Squadron as a flight commander in India – http://www.bbc.co.uk/ww2peopleswar/ stories/53/a6784653.shtml.

The book *Men of the Battle of Britain – A Biographical Directory of 'The Few'* by Kenneth G Wynn (CCB Associates, second edn, 1999) provided another brief biography.

Even before obtaining his service record it was possible to establish the bare bones of his RAF career using the online version of the *London Gazette* at http://www.london-gazette.co.uk/search.

With a date of birth and year of death it was a simple exercise to search the England and Wales Death Index on Ancestry which gave a reference for his death in January to March 1983 in the Uttersland district, vol. 9, p. 3755. Using this reference I obtained a copy of his death certificate from the General Register Office. With proof of death it was now possible to obtain part, at least, of Guy's RAF Service Record.

Obtaining Guy's Royal Air Force Service Record

The best way to obtain a service record for anyone who served in the RAF after the First World War is via the Veterans Agency website at http://www.veterans-uk.info/service_records/raf .html, which explains the rather complex rules and allows you to obtain the necessary Subject Access Request form and Certificate of Kinship form. The completed forms should be sent to: RAF Disclosures Section, Room 221b, Trenchard Hall, RAF Cranwell, Sleaford, Linconshire, NG34 8HB; tel: 01400 261201, ext 6711, ext 8161/8159 (officers), ext 8163/8168/8170 (other ranks). You should provide as many details of your relative as possible, especially their service number (if you have it), full name, date of birth and rank (if possible).

Under their rules, if the person has been dead for less than twenty-five years and you aren't next of kin (or have their written permission) the RAF will only provide surname; forename; rank; service number; regiment/corps; place of birth; age; date of birth; date of death where this occurred in service; the date an individual joined the service; the date of leaving; good conduct medals (i.e., Long Service and Good Conduct Medal (LS&GCM)), any orders of chivalry and gallantry medals (decorations of valour) awarded, some of which may have been announced in the *London Gazette*. After this period, and if it is held, the MOD will disclose without the requirement for next of kin consent: the units in which he/she served; the dates of this service and the locations of those units; the ranks in which the service was carried out and details of Second World War campaign medals.

Ancestry suggested Guy Marsland had died in Essex in the first quarter of 1983. Using a copy of his death certificate, I was able to obtain details of all his postings during his service, which proved to be only partly correct. The glaring error, which would have caused no end of problems, is the complete absence of any mention of his posting to 136 Squadron in Burma in February 1942 – the service record states that he continued with 137 Squadron for another ten months! If I hadn't already picked up from online sources the apparently reliable fact that he'd served in early 1942 with 136 Squadron, it would have meant tracing back from 224 Group ORB and forward from 137 Squadron records to fill the gap. Service records are NOT an infallible source!

When it came to tracing Guy's combats, knowing that TNA holds online copies of RAF combat reports from the Second World War in its Discovery section, it was simple to discover that there were three reports dating from October and November 1940. The squadron ORB made no mention of any other combats so I think I'm on solid ground with the ones quoted – though it must be pointed out that not all combat records survive. The only combat mentioned for which I can't (yet) find confirmation, is the claim for a Japanese fighter over Akyab on 23 March 1942 which is mentioned in an excellent book, *Those Other Eagles* by Christopher Shores. Mr Shores' reputation is well known and he's well respected and I'm happy to accept his authority for the claim.

Sorting though Guy's various postings while he was in India and Burma proved a time-consuming task and I'm still not convinced that my interpretation is 100 per cent accurate. He moved (often on temporary attachments) so frequently that only by ploughing through the movement orders, usually enclosed as appendixes to the unit ORB, was it possible to spot his short period in hospital and some of his short-term attachments. These are not recorded on his service record which was compiled in London on the basis of the information that reached them from India – obviously not all of it did.

The air war in the Far East is not as well served as perhaps it might be but a couple of books proved invaluable. *Take Mary to the Pictures – A Fighter Pilot in Burma 1941–1945*, by Alan 'Kit' Kitley (Coston, 2003), paints a vivid picture of life in 136 Squadron in the air war over Burma. *Bloody Shambles*, by Christopher Shores, Brian Cull and Yasuho Izawa, is a three-part history of the air war over South-East Asia and it's clear that Christopher Shores was at one time in close contact with Guy Marsland, who appears in one or two photographs.

Chapter 6

FROM THE NORTH-WEST FRONTIER TO SINGAPORE, FORTY YEARS IN THE RAF – ERNEST EDGAR CHAMBERS AND MARY CRAIG CHAMBERS

Ernest Edgar (Jerry) Chambers was born in 1917. He joined the 26th Halton Apprentice Entry RAF at the age of 15 in September 1932 and left as a Warrant Officer in April 1972, having seen active service on the North-West Frontier in the late 1930s and in the Malaya and Singapore debacle in 1942, as well as serving in India and at home during the war. He married Mary Craig Pearson, Women's Auxiliary Air Force (WAAF), while serving at RAF West Dreugh and though she was discharged when she fell pregnant with their first daughter, she accompanied him on his many post-war tours abroad, including his final posting, back to Singapore.

At the age of 12 Jerry decided he wanted to join the join the RAF as a Halton apprentice. However, coming from Portsmouth and with parents who had a naval background he encountered resistance (from his mother only), so at the age of 15 he took entrance exams for apprenticeships for the RN, HM Dockyard and RAF. The most stringent criteria was that of the RAF entrance exam. For some bizarre reason he completely failed the exams for the RN and Dockyard but came in the top few for selection for the RAF.

The Halton Apprentice Scheme for which Jerry qualified had been established in 1919 by Chief of the Air Staff Hugh Trenchard. Designed to take boys straight from school, the three-year course turned out highly skilled fitters (men who worked on engines) and riggers (men who worked on the airframe). The whole scheme was planned to produce a highly trained body of educated men who had the potential for a career in the RAF (including the option to become sergeant pilots or reach officer rank). On passing out of Halton the men would sign on for ten years' Regular service, with two years in the Reserve and with the option of extending their Regular service. Food, lodgings and kit were provided free and cadets under the age of 18 were paid 1s 6d per day. Apprentices worked in the classrooms and workshops

A young Edgar (Jerry) Chambers in the uniform of a Halton apprentice, c. 1933. (Photograph courtesy of Barbara Chambers)

from Monday to Friday, with games on Wednesday afternoon and drills and inspections on Saturday and church parade on Sunday. Cadets were allowed out of camp on Saturday and Sunday afternoons and on Wednesdays after sports. Collectively (and proudly) the cadets were known as 'Halton Brats', or 'Trenchard Brats'.

While at Halton Jerry won a boxing cup (as runner up, the family still have it) in the inter-wing boxing tournament for mosquito weight. He was the only one in his wing in that weight category and his opponent was a boxer. He didn't last very long! On completion of his training Jerry worked on Vickers Virginias and Handley Page Harrows with 214 Squadron based at RAF Boscombe Down and then RAF Scampton then volunteered for service overseas. He was posted to India in March 1938, initially to 60 Squadron based at Kohat on the North-West Frontier, flying the Westland Wapiti, a two-seater biplane multi-purpose aircraft that had been introduced in the late 1920s.

At the time of Jerry's arrival the squadron were taking part in the more or less annual air operations against militant tribesmen on the North-West Frontier, bombing villages and attacking hostile gatherings of tribesmen. During this period Jerry was a pall bearer to a crew who had come down in the tribal areas and was very upset about the mutilated bodies.

Flight Lieutenant (later Air Vice-Marshal) J M Cohu (27 Squadron), an officer who served on the North-West Frontier at about the same time as Jerry, recalled, in 1967, something of his days on the Frontier,

> First place must be given to a tribute to the NCO's and aircraftmen, the 'other ranks'. Their lot was a very hard one and yet the service they gave was the very best . . . Theirs was a tour of duty up to seven years straight, without home leave, without their wives and families except for a small minority, and without female companionship of any sort. In spite of these conditions they gave unstinting service and loyalty at all times . . . Living conditions were only as good as the times and the situation permitted. The heat in the hot season was a burden to be endured by all. Work started at dawn and finished about one pm when the temperature was near the hundred mark. Sleep at night under mosquito nets was often difficult, and sometimes a hellish wind off the desert sent the temperature as high as 115 degrees F.

At the end of April 1939 Ernest was posted to the Air Depot, India at RAF Drigh Road. 60 Squadron was converting to fly the Bristol Blenheim. Presumably, this detachment was to learn the basic details of servicing the new Blenheims that were beginning to arrive in India and which, with their monoplane construction, all-metal skin and retractable undercarriage, were a considerable change from the venerable Westland Wapiti. Following a three-month detachment to Drigh Road, Jerry was posted to 27 Squadron, which was also due to re-equip with Blenheims, at Risalpur. The first flight of Blenheims over the North-West Frontier Province took place in August 1939 but on the outbreak of war the squadron was ordered to form the nucleus of a flying training school and moved to Risalpur, though one flight of Wapitis did serve briefly at Bombay on coastal duties before returning to Risalpur in November.

Throughout 1940 the squadron continued in a training role, turning out pilots and navigators who trained on Tiger Moths and Hawker Harts before moving on to the Wapiti. In October 1940 the squadron was finally equipped with Blenheims and in early 1941 was ordered to Malaya.

Colin Chambers, Jerry's son, told me,

> There was a shortfall of Observers, as they were needed for the bomber offensive in Europe. The Squadron were given 4 Navigators straight out of training. Squadron Leader Hackett, asked for 'selected' volunteers to temporarily fill the role of navigators. My father was one of those volunteers.
>
> In February 1941 27 Squadron moved from India to Singapore, the aircraft flew in 3 flights of 4 aircraft. Each flight had a real navigator. During the transit my father's flight went into a cloud bank & when they came out of the other end, they were alone; he then had to draw on his limited navigational skills. They then hit another cloud bank & when they came out of it saw one of the other formations & joined it.

Though the squadron ORB has little information for late 1940 and early 1941, it does confirm that Jerry flew in Blenheim L8621 flown by Sergeant Pilot Kennedy, which left Risalpur on 13 February 1942 and arrived at Calcutta on the 14th. They then flew on to Akyab and from there to Alor Star in Malaya – it was on this leg of the flight that the aircraft ran into cloud and lost formation, with a couple of planes turning back, then to Mergui Road in Singapore.

The squadron was now stationed at the Singapore Civil Airport at Kallang. Unfortunately, Squadron Leader Hackett was killed at Kallang a short time after the move took place, and he was replaced by Squadron Leader F R C Fowle. While at Kallang the squadron trained as a fighter squadron using their Blenheim I aircraft and attempts were made to train them in night fighting. Colin told me:

> Shortly after arriving in Singapore he [Jerry] was promoted to Sergeant. He thoroughly enjoyed this period in the bright lights of Singapore. But it was marred by the loss Squadron Leader 'Sam' Hackett & his crew, when their aircraft span into

the sea. My father always spoke very highly of Sqn Ldr Hackett & regarded him as an inspirational leader.

In May 1941 the squadron moved to Butterworth in Burma's Wellesley Province, a new station still under construction. Here the squadron carried out a good number of interception exercises but there were problems with both the operations room which controlled the squadron from the ground and with wireless communication with the airborne aircraft. There were also exercises in formation flying and air to ground cooperation with the 4th Infantry Division. Colin says:

In May 27 Squadron moved north to Butterworth near Penang, the airfield was still under construction & the accommodation was a former leper colony. It was quite a pleasant location adjacent to a long sandy beach. This all changed in August when the Sqn moved again, this time to Sungei Patani which was yet another unfinished airfield with limited infrastructure, in a clearing carved out of a rubber plantation in the middle of nowhere, near the Thai border. In late November 21 Squadron Royal Australian Air Force (RAAF) moved up from Sembawang in Singapore to join 27 at Sungei Patani. The Australians were not impressed with their new home & relationships between the two squadrons were not good. In my father's words 'we had carved our dispersals out of the jungle, but they were quite happy to line up their Aircraft for photo shoots & wait for the locals to create some dispersals for them'.

21 Squadron RAAF brought with them Buffalo fighters and by early December the two squadrons were settled in. On the night 7/8 December news came through that the Japanese had bombed Singapore (at about the same time as they'd attacked Pearl Harbor) and that landings were reported at Kota Bahru. On the morning of 8 December the squadron mounted its first operational sortie, bombing and strafing Japanese landing craft at Kota Bahru. Finding few targets, the main Japanese force of cruiser, several destroyers and eight transports having sailed north, they returned to Sangei Patani. On their return they discovered that the aerodrome had been badly bombed.

A report by Wing Commander W F Allshorn, written in 1946,

describes the raid from the point of view of 21 Squadron (RAAF). They were warned that hostilities with Japan had commenced at 0130 hours on 8 December and that the Japanese were bombing Singapore. Squadron Leader Fowle, Station Commander, conferred with Allshorn and the senior flight commander of 27 Squadron and it was decided to prepare the Buffalos for defensive and reconnaissance work at dawn. As a result, twelve aircraft were prepared and ready at 0630 hours and the crews were briefed with the limited information available. Squadron Leader Fowle personally took over the station operations room.

At 0700 hours Fowle telephoned the 21 Squadron (RAAF) briefing room to advise that two enemy aircraft were approaching and ordered that one section was to stand by and await instructions. Two aircraft were warmed up by the ground staff. At 0710 five aircraft in close formation were sighted almost overhead at 11,000ft. A call to the ops room received the instruction to 'stand by for further instruction'. Simultaneously, the 21 Squadron pilots realised the planes were Japanese Mitsubishi 97 Bombers and dashed for their aircraft. Allshorn recalls, 'As the 12 pilots were putting on parachutes and the aircraft were being warmed I looked up to see a stick of bombs leave the enemy formation and I realised that it was too late to take off'. Under orders from Allshorn most of the pilots and ground crew took cover, though the two pilots who were already with their aircraft managed to take off. Some thirty-five or forty bombs fell among, or close to, the aircraft on the stand-by (they had not been dispersed and were lined up close together) and another stick hit the station HQ (killing two operators and destroying station communications) and a small fuel dump. A sixteen-strong party of female Chinese workers were all killed. Of the twelve stand-by aircraft, seven were rendered unserviceable by fire or bomb fragments. The two Buffalos that had got airborne returned having attempted to attack the Japanese, only to find their guns did not function. They landed between the bomb craters. Presumably, at some point after this, the Blenheims returning from their attack at Kota Bahru also landed.

At 1045 hours a formation of fifteen or so aircraft was seen approaching from the same direction at about 12,000ft. Allshorn recalls, 'Station Operations Room Controller, Squadron Leader Fowl [*sic*], again refused to allow 21 Squadron aircraft to take off on request.' Two sticks of bombs were dropped; one hit and destroyed a large petrol dump and the other damaged the barracks as well as further damaging the airfield itself, almost prohibiting it from further use. 27 Squadron must have suffered casualties in this attack as both it and 21 Squadron (RAAF) were later noted as having only four serviceable aircraft left at the end of the day and that morale among the squadron personnel was badly affected. Again, Allshorn recalls, 'Their helplessness on the scantily protected aerodromes in the face of severe and constant bombing and machine gun attacks, during which aircraft were remorselessly destroyed without replacement, had its due effect.' The local labourers on the airfield defected en masse and rumours of disasters in the land fighting were circulating. An army intelligence officer was subsequently arrested and sent to Singapore charged with providing the Japanese with information about the airfields which it was thought had allowed them to bomb the airfield so opportunely, and with circulating the rumours. According to Jerry Chambers, the casualties to 21 Squadron RAAF planes were caused because they were still lined up on the aerodrome and no attempt had been made to disperse them.

As a consequence of the attacks, both squadrons, with their personnel, were withdrawn to Butterworth, where problems with morale continued. Allshorn recalls, 'There was no senior RAF officer at Butterworth with sufficient weight to take control and there was no doubt that some personnel got out of hand. It should be made clear, however, that loss of morale applied only to personnel evacuated from Sungei Patani viz. Nos 21 (F) (RAAF) and 27 (NF) Squadrons, particularly no 21.' A Court of Enquiry was convened to investigate the circumstances and a preliminary report submitted, which was subsequently lost. After the war the President of the Court, Group Captain McCauley (RAAF), recalled that the general findings were that 'while the planning and control of the evacuation was not up to the desired standard and there was lack of coordination between Squadron and Station Commanders, the evidence did not reveal any instance where disciplinary action was called for against any individual'.

According to Jerry, the Australians evacuated without orders from the station commander (who complained that they'd 'buggered off') taking almost all the motorised transport, including the fuel bowsers, with them. At this stage 27 Squadron still had twelve Blenheims (one twin sicker on sticks), eleven aircraft in various states of disrepair with one Blenheim lost (this aircraft was lost when the sergeant pilot attempted to take off to intercept the second raid and was hit by a bomb on take-off). 27 Squadron was then ordered to withdraw to Butterworth by Norgroup. The aircraft on sticks was destroyed as it was unrecoverable in the timescale available and eleven Blenheims then flew south to Butterworth.

According to Colin,

My Father and a few 'selected' men were then sent to the local town to 'requisition' transport to replace that acquired by 21 Sqn. All of the party were given Tommy guns, which none of them knew how to use, which was fortunate as they had no ammo. On return to base with said vehicles, he was deemed to be a natural leader of men. (At this point it needs to mentioned that my Dad was not the Engineering Officer's favourite.) He was selected to run a rear party. Having brought the vehicles back to Sungei Patani, the Sqn ground crew moved south, with the exception of a rear party (Guess Who), who were left to recover spares etc.

27 Sqn arrived at Butterworth with 11 Blenheims. 81 Repair & Salvage unit moved north & with the rear party of 27, recovered as many spares as they could in the vehicles available & destroyed the rest. They then moved south to Butterworth, when they arrived there, the airfield had been hit by 2 raids, which had reduced 27 Sqn to 4 aircraft. 21 Squadron RAAF had already left southbound, but for some inexplicable reason had forgotten four of their aircraft.

These Buffaloes were made flyable & refuelled by 81 R & SU & 27 Sqn rear party. They then had to find 4 Blenheim pilots to fly them south. The pilots were a mix & match of 27 & 61 Sqn and my father said one of them was his friend Jock Kennedy (by this time a Flight Sergeant). They had limited info on the aircraft, they knew how to retract the undercart, but not how to get it down again. 4 Buffaloes were successfully flown from Butterworth to Singapore, with their undercart down all the way (probably arriving before their intended pilots, who had chosen to leave by road).

Over the next couple of days 27 Squadron flew few patrols over Wellesley Province. In a brief letter from a pilot in 27 Squadron in

1942 it is recorded that, 'the Blenheim fighter was little match for the Navy Zeros or Army 97's. Fortunately, casualties were light although many aircraft were lost on the ground. Attempts were made to escort Blenheim Mk IV's on raids over Siam, with indifferent success.' (AIR 27/5578 – 'Malaya operations 1941–1942: fighter operations').

On 12 December the squadron, which had no serviceable aircraft and probably only five airworthy ones, was ordered to Tengeh aerodrome on Singapore island where it was absorbed into the Bomber Pool. On 15 December the squadron was moved to Kallang, the fighter aerodrome for Singapore where it was re-formed into a night-fighter squadron (according to Jerry Chambers, by the simple expedient of painting them black). Japanese night raids were achieving little damage but were a constant nuisance. The squadron had managed to get five Blenheims serviceable but they had no success due to the poor performance of the aircraft.

Between 23 and 27 January 1942 the main body of 27 Squadron personnel were evacuated by ship to Sumatra, leaving behind a small aircraft handling party for the remaining Blenheims. This was headed by Jerry Chambers, who was chosen for the role by his 'best mate', the engineering officer. Colin explained,

All of the recoverable aircraft at Kallang were sorted & the rest of 27 Squadron then left for Sumatra. My father then took his team to Tengah on the North of Singapore island & offered his services to the Station Commander. Group Captain 'Poppa' Watts. He went straight to the Station commander even though he was a very young Sergeant, because he had seen breakdowns in the chain of command over the previous months. At a time when large numbers of RAF personnel were leaving at speed, he and his men were repairing damaged aircraft that were subsequently flown to Sumatra. Poppa Watts was there several times every day to check up on their needs.

At the beginning of the 2nd week of Feb 1941, my Dad went back to Poppa Watts & told him that they had recovered every aircraft they could. He was thanked & told that He & his men would be on the next ship to Sumatra. His word was his bond & I believe shortly after this Poppa Watts shot himself as he did not want to be taken prisoner. My father was gutted when he found out some years later what had happened.

Group Captain Frank Eric Watts (whose date of death is given, perhaps mistakenly, as 4 February 1942) is commemorated on the Singapore Memorial at Kranji War Cemetery.

By 10 February the situation in Singapore had become critical. The Assistant Air Officer Commanding, Air Vice-Marshal Maltby, was sent by air to Sumatra to take command of the RAF units there. Air Vice-Marshal Pulford also ordered the evacuation of all remaining RAF personnel and this began the next day. Aerodrome surfaces were ploughed up and as much equipment that could not be evacuated as possible was destroyed or rendered useless. On 13 February, having ensured the evacuation of as many RAF personnel as he could, Air Vice-Marshal Pulford attempted to reach Sumatra by sea but died in the attempt. On 15 February Singapore surrendered. Colin recalls,

On arrival at Palembang, my father took his team to P2 [an airfield believed to be unknown to the Japanese], when he arrived at the airfield he bumped into Jock Kennedy, who told him that the squadron was about to withdraw to Java & that they were arranging a rear party to head north to Medan, to refuel & rearm replacement aircraft coming from India (which never arrived). Jock Kennedy said to my father, I suggest you take your men back into the Ulu (Jungle) & come back in a couple of hours, otherwise it's going to be you lot again. My father did as was suggested & said that he felt awful about those who were sent North, but his responsibility was for his men who been abandoned by the Squadron in Singapore.

When he reappeared at P2, the men had been sent North & he & his men joined the Squadron moving south to Ooesthaven by train, mostly on flatbeds. What was left of the Squadron were sent from one airfield to another & some attacks were carried out, which whittled away the remaining aircraft. The remnants of 27 were then ordered to withdraw to Tjilitjap, on the south coast of Java to be evacuated. When they arrived there, the port was in a state of chaos. There was an embryonic embarkation unit, but insufficient ships to evacuate all the personnel.

On 26 February, as many RAF personnel as could be crammed aboard were evacuated from Java on the vessel *Khota Gede*, bound for Freemantle in Western Australia. Those who got a place were determined by a very draconian system of 'how long will it take to train your replacement'. Aircrew and fitters (depending on seniority and experience) were given a place. Others were left behind, with a representative number of officers of all levels. Those left behind were eventually rounded up by the Japanese and spent (those that survived) the remainder of the war as POWs.

The convoy set sail and headed south-west. During the first night, the RAF officers on board spoke to the Captain and convinced him that the personnel on board were needed in India to fight the next Japanese offensive. Another airman, who also escaped on the *Khota Gede*, described the voyage, and this is featured on the BBC WW2 People's War website,

> We found ourselves on the 'Kota Gede' – 'Big Fort' in Malay – a tramp streamer of some 2500 tons, with room, perhaps for 6 passengers. What a bastion she was to the 2000 or more airmen crammed aboard her for the next nine days. She did not have facilities to cope with the large number on board but there were no complaints. The captain was Fredrick Goos, the crew mixed one of Dutch and Indonesians.
>
> Two queues stretched right round the ship, one forward and one aft twice a day for meals of bully beef and stew. The only 'plates' were slices of bread and 'cups' were tin cans. There was the luxury of bread and rice pudding during the early part of the voyage. The only fresh water was for cooking.
>
> There were a number of deaths on board, the bodies being slipped into the sea after a few words from the padre. To keep out of the lanes of Japanese bombers and submarines the Captain steered SSW until Sunday 1 March when he changed to NNW. He had been ordered to sail in convoy style to Australia but he decided to head for Ceylon. At the end of the war Captain Goos was expecting to be court-martialled but when the facts were known he was decorated for having saved his ship and at least 2000 servicemen.
>
> At Colombo in Ceylon we transferred to the 'Dunera', hoping we were returning to the UK but in fact arriving in Bombay and then Karachi.
>
> Against orders the Captain set sail across the Indian Ocean

Mary Pearson (fourth from left, front row) on her initial training course, 1941.
(Photograph courtesy of Barbara Chambers)

and arrived at Colombo in early March with 2,500 well-trained, battle-experienced aircrew and ground crew.

Sergeant Chambers was posted immediately to No. 28 Squadron, a Lysander squadron that was reforming at Lahore having lost most of its aircraft in the retreat through Burma. For most of 1942 the squadron was based on the North-West Frontier, taking part in army exercises. In July 1942 Jerry was posted back to Britain and, on his return on 8 August, was posted to a flying training school at RAF Hullavington and then to No. 4 Air Observer School at RAF West Freugh, near Stranraer, part of No. 29 Group of Flying Training Command.

Jerry Chambers as Sergeant Fitter.
(Photograph courtesy of Barbara Chambers)

95

As a sergeant fitter (he was promoted to flight sergeant in December 1944), Jerry was in charge of the maintenance of aircraft in a particular hangar, with a squad of fitters and riggers under him. He remained at West Freugh until the end of the war, though it was renamed No. 4 (Observer) Advanced Flying Unit. It was here that he met his future wife, Mary.

Mary Craig Pearson was born on 2 December 1920 at Dunbar, East Lothian. She'd enlisted (she was not a conscript) into the WAAF on 17 June 1941 giving her civilian occupation as shop assistant. After her basic training and a spell at No. 1 Motor Transport School, Blackpool, then the Equipment Training School (Airmen) where she was taught her trade, she was posted to RAF West Freugh. Here she was an equipment assistant in servicing stores, handing out small parts for aircraft parts and had to know what the parts were, not just their numbers. She also had to make out vouchers for larger parts, get them signed by the squadron leader and sent to the maintenance unit. If an aeroplane was held up waiting for parts the voucher had to have AOG on it ('Aircraft on Ground'). She also made the tea for the senior NCOs in charge of the different hangars – which was not part of her job, but they all congregated there for their tea. There was an airman who worked with her called Mac, who ran errands,

Group shot of the maintenance crew at RAF West Freugh. Mary Pearson is far left, bottom row and Jerry Chambers is seated sixth from right, second row. (Photograph courtesy of Barbara Chambers)

collected parts from main stores and who she sent to scrounge the tea from the cookhouse. Squadron Leader Lindley was in charge and very protective of 'his WAAF'. If Mary was going home for the weekend, he would ring up the guardroom on the Friday to say that she would be leaving early so she could make her train connections – you weren't supposed to leave camp before 5pm.

The authorities had no problem with an NCO and a leading aircraftswoman courting, but, as daughter Barbara tells me, 'after they had been going out for a while Dad was called in to see the WAAF Officer who asked him if his intentions were honourable'. They married at the Abbey Church in Dunbar on 18 September 1944 and continued to work together. On 2 April 1945 Mary was given a compassionate discharge from the WAAF because she was preg-

Jerry and Mary's wedding at the Abbey Church, Dunbar, 18 September 1944. (Photograph courtesy of Barbara Chambers)

nant with daughter Barbara. Mary's service record shows that she had consistently been graded as 'Very Good' in terms of Character and 'Superior' in Trade Proficiency. Their marriage continued happily until Jerry's death on 9 April 1995 with Mary (and growing family) following Jerry on his many postings abroad. Daughter Barbara tells me, 'She definitely thinks having been in the service made it easier as she knew what to expect, and before they got married Dad told her that there might be times when the air force had to come first.'

With the end of the war in Europe Jerry stayed at West Freugh for a while with the Care and Maintenance Party then was posted to 57 Maintenance Unit. In 1946 he was posted to 615 Squadron Royal Auxiliary Air Force at Biggin Hill and in 1949 to 502 Squadron Royal Auxiliary Air Force.

In 1951 he was posted to the Middle East Air Force, to RAF Fayid in Egypt. This was a troubled period in Egypt, with anti-British riots. Daughter Barbara recalls,

> Mum, Jill and I had quite an adventure when we went out to Egypt. We sailed in the *Empress of Australia* in 1951, but while we were en route there was trouble in Egypt. After we had

Part of the Care and Maintenance Party at RAF West Freugh, 1945. (Photograph courtesy of Barbara Chambers)

landed the troops and ferried some more from Cyprus, we, plus some of the families already there were sent home again on the same ship. It made the pathe news and newspapers when we landed back at Liverpool. We eventually went out again on the *Empire Fowey* in December 1952 and had Christmas on board.

After two-and-a-half years' service abroad Jerry (who had already extended his original twelve years' service by an additional twelve years) served at home in a series of flying training schools including 2 FTS at RAF Hullavington and 7 FTS at RAF Valley on Anglesey. In 1958 he was posted to RAF Wildenrath in West Germany where 88 Squadron were equipped with Canberra jet light bombers and 17 Squadron with Canberra reconnaissance aircraft. Though he'd originally trained on propeller-driven radial engine aircraft, Jerry had retrained on jet engines in 1955. Being, as it were, on the front line in the Cold War, exercises were held regularly involving sudden alerts and simulated raids against Britain to test the fighter defences. The station ORB mentions many of these in detail, including Operation Flashback, in September 1960, when the station was assumed to have been the target of an atomic bomb at the start of the exercise,

> The atomic strike provided an excellent opportunity to fully exercise the Damage Control Unit and the opportunity was seized almost avidly by the Directing Staff to provide some difficult situations. These ranged from the destruction of all messing facilities on the station to despatching a body of men to dispose of a group of saboteurs etc at a nearby railway station. These activities were played out against the continual background of clicking Geiger Counters etc as radiological monitoring teams roamed far and wide around the station.

It was a long way from pursuing tribal troublemakers on the North-West Frontier!

Jerry was in Germany for three years before another spell in Britain, once again posted to flying training schools, before being posted to RAF Near East Air Force based on Cyprus but also covering the RAF in Libya. He served first at RAF El Adem in what was then the Kingdom of Libya. Situated near Tobruk, it does not seem to have been a popular posting, located as it was on the edge of the desert. For Jerry and Mary it may not have been so bad – Barbara Chambers recalls that 'When in Libya, they did not live at El Adem, but in a bungalow in Tobruk among the Libyan people. There was a Captain and his family from the King's Guard living in the adjoining bungalow who they were friendly with and King Idris' palace was just down the road.' El Adem's role was mainly as a transit point for flights to Cyprus, the Sudan and points East and a former airman posted there at about the same time as Jerry recalls on his website,

> This more often than not was a refuelling stop or a crew slipping point, Britannias from 99/511 Squadron, Comets from 216 squadron, Hastings from 24 and 36 Squadrons, Argosies from RAF Benson, Shackletons from various stations, Beverleys, Vulcans some with Blue Steel bombs on board, Hunters, Javelins and the list is almost endless including civilian aircraft, several of which would be carrying pilgrims to the Haj at Mecca. Somehow or other we had to turn this little lot round to see them on their next leg of their journey, we were all specialists in our own field, there was always someone that had worked on one of the kites that would come through and

Group photograph taken at RAF El Adem, Libya. (Photograph courtesy of Barbara Chambers)

if there was a 'snag' [technical problem] that someone didn't know we could always ask the Flight Engineer or consult with the 'bible' the Air Publication for that aircraft.

After a year in Libya Jerry was posted to RAF Akrotiri, on Cyprus, with 73 Squadron, another Canberra squadron. The service record mentions a brief, two-month attachment to RAF Tengeh in Malaya, possibly connected with the basing there of 9 Squadron's Vulcan bombers, which passed through Akrotiri on their way East as part of a deterrent force against Indonesian aggression in the area. After a brief spell at RAF Hal Far on Malta and more time with 73 Squadron on Cyprus, Jerry returned to Britain in December 1966 to serve at RAF Lyneham in Wiltshire.

For his final posting before taking retirement Jerry was offered the posting of his choice. He chose Singapore and spent four happy years there before returning to Britain. Son Colin was with him and recalls one final, poignant memory, 'In 1968 My Dad was posted to Changi in Singapore, the following year we went to Kranji Cemetery. My father stared at the wall with all the names of those who had died as POWs. My Mother pulled me to one side; it was the first time I had seen my Father cry.'

Jerry finally retired from the RAF when he was 55, in 1972, having extended his service yet again. In his career he was awarded the General Service Medal with Bar for the North-West Frontier, the Pacific Star, the 1939–45 Medal, the Defence Medal and the Long Service and Good Conduct Medal.

Researching Jerry and Mary Chambers

Though Jerry died in 1995, Mary is still alive and was able to obtain her own service record and, as Jerry's next of kin, his record too. Both were complete and free of charge (for details of obtaining service records see Chapter 5).

For the most part the service records are clear, but in Jerry's case there are problems for parts of his service during 1942 and 1943. His movements for the period after 27 Squadron went to Malaya are unclear. Given the circumstances this is hardly surprising, but even after his return to India there's no mention of his posting to 28 Squadron. Happily, he'd mentioned it to his son Colin, who passed the information on to me and, in the Appendices to 28 Squadron's

ORB (AIR 27/235) there is a list of ground crew which includes his name.

For the period with 27 Squadron itself one would normally turn to the squadron ORB – unfortunately for historians, later events meant that some portions for the period were lost, leaving gaps that read: 'These records were destroyed at Singapore when the Squadron was lost. A new Squadron was formed in September 1942 in India.'

Fortunately, the RAF compiled reports after the war, drawing on the memories of surviving participants and the limited available records. Some of the memories slightly contradict others (hardly surprising after five years of war) but it is possible to trace the general movements of the squadron and confirm, generally, the stories Colin provided me. Certainly, I've seen nothing that contradicts anything that Jerry told him and I'm happy to trust the stories. Records used include AIR 20/5578: 'Malaya operations 1941–1942: fighter operations'; AIR 23/2123: 'Operations of the R.A.F. during the campaigns in Malaya and Netherlands East Indies: report by Air Vice-Marshal P.C. Maltby'; AIR 29/804: 'REPAIR AND SALVAGE UNITS No. 81 Seletar and Kluang'; AIR 20/12344: 'Java: various operations; AIR 20/2117: Singapore: air defence'.

For Jerry's post-war squadrons and stations the ORBs are in AIR 27 (for squadrons) and AIR 28 series as for his Second World War service. The station ORB for El Adem, for example, is in AIR 28/1575 and the ORB for 73 Squadron is in AIR 27/2950, AIR 27/2951 and AIR 27/3101.

One bright point about Jerry's later career, reaching, as it does, into the early 1970s, is the number of websites that have been set up by RAF veterans who served in the same squadrons or on the same bases. For RAF El Adem, for example, there's an interesting website created by another RAF man who served there at http://splashdown2.tripod.com/theroyalairforce/id6.html.

Chapter 7

AN AUSTRALIAN AIR GUNNER WITH BOMBER COMMAND – VICTOR CHARLES REID

Large numbers of foreigners served with the RAF during the Second World War, including thousands from the Empire. One was Victor

Charles Reid, a grazier from New South Wales (NSW), who flew thirty-one missions with 15 Squadron and was awarded the Distinguished Flying Cross. He participated in the Battle of Berlin, the disastrous Nuremberg raid and attacks over France.

Born on 7 December 1914 at Triamble, NSW, Vic voluntarily enlisted (the Government could only conscript men for Home Service) in Sydney on 28 March 1942. He joined the Royal Australian Air Force (RAAF) at No. 2 Recruitment Centre in Sydney 'for the duration of the war and a period of twelve months thereafter'.

A November 1939 agreement had established the Empire Air

Sergeant Vic Reid, RAAF. (Courtesy of Martyn Ford-Jones)

Training Scheme whereby basic training was completed in Australia before posting for service with the RAF or RAAF. The RAAF established 2 air navigation schools, 3 air observers schools, 3 bombing and gunnery schools, 12 Elementary Flying Training Schools, 6 initial flying training schools and 8 service flying training schools. A further 7 schools of technical training and other specialised technical schools instructed ground crews in the maintenance of aircraft and equipment. Vic was one of 15,746 Australians who saw service with the RAF; a further 11,641 serving with RAAF squadrons.

Vic was immediately posted to No. 2 Initial Training School at RAAF Bradfield Park at Lindfield, NSW. Here he received his basic training and assessments and was considered good enough for aircrew so received some training in navigation and aerodynamics. On 8 June he was posted to 2 Wireless Air Gunnery School at Parkes, NSW, then to 2 Bombing and Air Gunnery School at Port Pirie, South Australia, on 12 December 1942. He qualified as an air gunner and was promoted to temporary sergeant. After nearly three months' training he was posted to No. 2 Embarkation Depot back at Bradfield Park for his final medical and kitting out, then to No. 1 Embarkation Depot at Ascot Vale, Melbourne, to sail to Britain.

Arriving in Britain in April 1943 he was first posted to No. 11 Personnel Despatch and Reception Centre (PDRC) at Brighton and Charmy Down, a centre especially created for RAAF arrivals and departures. He was there until 4 May 1943 when he was posted to No. 26 Operational Training Unit to commence his operational training. Here he flew 86 hours in Wellington Bombers on training exercises where each crew member would learn their individual role as part of the team. As an air gunner Vic would have learned more about gun turrets, machine guns and how to keep watch for attacking enemy aircraft.

In early August Vic was posted to 1651 Conversion Unit to be specifically trained in flying Stirling Bombers and after a month was posted to 620 Squadron, a Stirling squadron that had been involved in night-bombing operations throughout the summer. He was there only a fortnight before being posted to 1657 Conversion Unit.

After six weeks, on 4 November 1943, Vic was posted to 15 Squadron, a Regular bomber squadron with a fine tradition going back to the First World War. It had suffered terrible casualties in

May 1940 flying Blenheims, attacking the German advance into Belgium and Holland. Re-equipping with Wellington Bombers, then with the four-engined Stirling, they'd taken part in the Thousand Bomber raid to Cologne in May 1942. They'd flown more raids than any other Stirling squadron and (with 218 Squadron) had suffered the heaviest casualties. In December 1943 the squadron was stood down while it re-equipped again, this time with the Lancaster Bomber. Vic, who was now a flight sergeant, was assigned as a crew member to Flight Sergeant Alan Amies (pilot) as Mid Upper Gunner and was joined by two men who'd been at 620 Squadron with him, Flight Sergeant Eddy Orchard as Rear Gunner and Flight Sergeant Richard 'Basher' Hearne as Flight Engineer.

Their first operational raid (and first Lancaster raid for the squadron) was against Brunswick on 14 January 1944. A dozen aircraft from 15 Squadron were assigned to the raid, though only nine took part in what was not a great success, most of the bombs falling in open country. The squadron ORB records the crew's experience: 'Cloud over target. Skymarkers bombed. Neither flak or fighters gave any trouble, but 4000 lb bomb brought back due to failure in electrical circuit.' A week later they attacked Magdeburg as part of a 648 aircraft raid, the first on this target. Once again there was little damage to the town, in part because some aircraft arrived before the Pathfinders and attacked on their own initiative. Some aircraft continued to bomb the fires caused, though Amies' crew reported '5/10 clouds over target. Ground visible, but sky markers attacked. One big explosion seen, green in colour. Little opposition.' The last part is curious, as Bomber Command suffered their heaviest casualties of the war so far but possibly this reflects the isolation of each aircraft which could only report the tiny bit of the battle that was its own. Flying, not in formation, but as part of a bomber stream, it was quite possible to fly an entire operation and scarcely see another aircraft.

On 30 January the crew made their first raid on Berlin, the German capital and repeated target for Bomber Command. The city had been attacked two nights before and fifteen times before that since August 1943. Though extensive damage had been done and hundreds of casualties caused, the air defences were still functioning well. The target was completely clouded over and the aircraft were dependent upon the Pathfinders to locate and mark the target. Amies' crew noted the thick cloud and 'Bombed skymarkers, but results difficult to see. Spoof fighter flares were seen. By the glow on the clouds results should be good.'

A fortnight later they were briefed for another Berlin raid (15 February) but jettisoned some of their bomb load and turned back when the rear turret failed. On the 19th they attacked Leipzig recording, '10/10 cloud obscured target, but TIs & skymarkers were good and bombed the latter. Route markers were also good. Small glow beneath cloud indicated fires.' 15 Squadron was part of No. 3 Bomber Group and the group report on the raid says, 'This was another attack through 10/10ths cloud which, in spite of the number of crews arriving very early, owing, apparently, to allowing for a wind that was non-existent, on one of the legs, turned out to be quite a good attack.' Whatever the result of the raid, it was another bad night for Bomber Command, losing 79 aircraft out of 921 sorties (not all against Leipzig) mostly to German night fighters who got into the bomber stream early.

On 20 February the target was the southern German industrial city of Stuttgart, the crew reporting, 'Cloud was 7/10 over target. Bombed good concentration of skymarkers. Fires visible through gaps in cloud & one big explosion seen at 0413 hrs. Results appeared to be good.' The raid report doesn't mention an attack on the aircraft on the return journey. The combat report submitted by Amies describes the attack,

> Our aircraft was on the homeward journey, when the captain saw a Me. 110 climbing to attack on the port beam, range about 250 yds. He immediately put the nose down and turned into the attack, and four bursts of tracer from the attacking aircraft passed over the tailplanes of our aircraft. The enemy aircraft then turned and broke away on the port quarter, the rear gunner getting in a burst just before the E/A was lost. No claims. Rounds fired from rear turret – 50.

No. 3 Group was pleased with the result of the raid, saying,

> The attack on this target turned out to be more successful than the first impressions indicated. The attack was carried out over cloud that varied between 3/10ths and 10/10ths. The sky markers and marker bombs were well placed, resulting in the centre of the city receiving damage, while the main weight of

the attack fell on the industrial suburbs. This, for a long time, has been the most elusive target and considerable chagrin has been felt that the Bosch Works and the Daimler Benz Factory had previously escaped comparatively lightly. At last these two works have been hit badly, and it is expected that their recovery will be slow and a painful thorn in the side of German War Production Chiefs.

On 24 February the target was the Schweinfurt ball and roller bearing factories, the destruction of which, 3 Group commented, 'would have catastrophic effects on the Hun's aircraft and tank production'. Though the crew's report says, 'Good visibility with a ground mist made it possible to see fires burning well, and it could be seen 100 miles away. Bombed Red TIs, which were in good concentration, and routemarkers were good', 3 Group were less impressed saying, 'The bombing was not of a high order, though some concentration was achieved in the very small built up area. The usual fields however received more than their share of bombs – but they can take it!'

On 1 March 15 Squadron was back over Stuttgart, which was covered with 10/10 cloud with few breaks. Though bombing was scattered, much damage was done to the city's important motor works. On 22 March the squadron attacked Frankfurt as part of a raid by 816 aircraft. The crew reported, 'fires seemed well concentrated. Jettisoned some incendiaries at 5215N 0830E and some around the searchlight belt on the way out.' A raid 36 hours later by American B17s, combined with this raid and one earlier in the month, caused the Germans to record that Frankfurt had practically ceased to exist.

On 24 March Bomber Command made its last major attack on Berlin. The crew reported, 'Early in attack and difficult to judge results. Bombed Red TIs through 5/10 cloud, but fires seemed to be spread over wide area.' 3 Group agreed with the crew's assessment, noting that,

An unfortunate night, due mainly to our old enemy, the weather. Wind velocities up to 120 mph were found by H2 aircraft on the way to the target; these were thought to be unreliable as they were nearly double forecast winds. As a result, many aircraft were blown off course, while others overshot badly. Bombing was scattered, but a considerable percentage of the bomb loads found Berlin and great credit is due to the many crews who made the best of a bad job. One crew identified themselves as over Leipzig, returned to Berlin, and bombed 40 minutes late. Raid commentators helped to centre the raid by 'pulling in' many aircraft who would otherwise have overshot the target. Many fighters were active, both in the target area and along the return route. Searchlights were very active.

On 30 March 1944 Vic and the crew took part in the raid that produced Bomber Command's heaviest casualties of the war. The target was Nuremberg and it was originally hoped that high cloud would cover the moon. Even when it was realised that it wouldn't the raid wasn't cancelled. Of the 795 aircraft despatched, 95 were shot down. The city was barely damaged.

The crew report made no mention of the casualties suffered and, taken in isolation, there's no indication that there were problems, 'Incendiaries burning short of aiming point and some a/c appeared to attack Schweinfurt. Skymarkers seen but bombed Red TIs through 7/10 cloud, & three separate areas of fires were visible. All routemarkers were seen.' The group report is more explicit:

This, the last attack of the month, met with determined fighter opposition; the most outstanding feature was the ease with which the enemy found our main bomber stream just south of Cologne. Many of our aircraft were reported to be making condensation trails, and these, clearly visible in the moonlight, may considerably have assisted the large number of enemy fighters which have been vectored into the stream. Many of our aircraft were seen to have been shot down in this area, though on the remainder of the route and over the target itself, opposition was slight.

On 11 April the target was Aachen and the group report recorded,

This, the first German target for the month, received an attack which appeared more scattered than usual. This was due, in part, to wind being lighter than expected, with the result that a few crews arrived early at the target. However, later reports show that the attack was successful. There was a good concentration in the marshalling yards and further damage was done to the town itself, which can now be considered virtually destroyed. Flak was poor and few fighters were encountered.

On 20 April the crew bombed Cologne, reporting, 'Unexpected winds caused a late arrival on the target, where Red skymarkers were seen and attacked. Markers disappeared into cloud too quickly. Good glow beneath cloud.' 3 Group considered the results overall had been good: 'The bombing was a bit scattered but heavy damage in the important industrial districts of EHNRENFELD and GERSON is confirmed by photographs. The GERSON marshalling yard is also heavily damaged. Flak was not up to standard, but enemy fighters were very active over the target and on the homeward route.'

On 22 April they were part of a 596-aircraft raid on Düsseldorf which caused widespread damage and killed over 1,000 people. The group reported,

A very good attack – TIs were seen to be concentrated on the marshalling yards. Many fires spread throughout the city and one large explosion was reported. A few undershoots were observed . . . but, in the main, the bombing was good. Flak and searchlights, slight at first, increased as the attack developed. Fighters were numerous and their work was simplified by the many contrails at 20,000 ft.

On the night of 12 May, Alan Amies, now a flight lieutenant and a popular and capable pilot, was asked to take a rookie crew on their first raid, against the

Flight Lieutenant Alan Amies, Vic Reid's pilot for his early raids. He was shot down and killed taking a rookie crew to Louvain in May 1944. (Courtesy of Martyn Ford-Jones)

railway yards at Louvain (now Leuven) in Belgium. Near the target they were intercepted by Oberleutnant Hans-Heinz Augenstein, a night fighter 'ace' who was to score a total of 46 'kills' during his career before himself being shot down later in the year. The Lancaster crashed north of Louvain, killing the entire crew, who are buried together in Leuven Communal Cemetery.

The loss of Amies, which must have been keenly felt by his normal crew, meant that they were now assigned as crew to Flight Lieutenant Oliver Brooks. Brooks had just been recommended for the Distinguished Flying Cross for bringing home his aircraft after it had been severely damaged in the Düsseldorf raid of 22 April. Attacked by a night fighter as he completed his bombing run, his port wing was hit. Brooks managed to turn away from the attack, only for a heavy flak shell to explode immediately below his open bomb doors. The blast tore through the aircraft, killing his bomb aimer almost immediately and mortally wounding his wireless operator. Unable to jump, because several parachutes had been damaged in the blast, Brooks nursed his aircraft through the searchlights and back across the North Sea at 500ft. With no undercarriage and his buckled bomb doors still open, he made a long approach to the special runway at RAF Woodbridge, created for such emergencies. He landed in a screech of metal and the plane skidded to a halt; the dead bodies were removed and the rest of the crew carried by ambulance to the sick bay. After a leave period Brooks was in need of a new crew and some of the late Amies' crew, including Vic, transferred to him.

Targets for the squadron, and indeed much of Bomber Command, were now switching away from Germany itself (though attacks there continued) to France and Belgium as the invasion approached. The raid on Louvain in which Amies was killed had been against railway yards and on 19 May Brooks and his new crew attacked the yards at Le Mans where they, 'Bombed Green TIs on instruction from Master bomber, but there was considerable R/T interference. The river and some ground detail could be identified and bombing appeared well concentrated.' The attack was successful, the locomotive sheds were destroyed, some ammunition waggons exploded, power lines were brought down and the two main lines were destroyed.

On 21 May they attacked Duisberg, where, despite cloud cover, they were able to bomb accurately thanks to good marking by the

Pathfinders and next night they took part in a mine-dropping operation, laying mines over the target area near Lim Fiord from
13,000ft.

On 30 May they took part in a thirty-nine-aircraft raid on a gun
battery at Boulogne and next night attacked the railway yards at
Trappes, reporting, 'Yellow spot fires which were pronounced by
the M/C as "Bang on" were attacked and a good concentration of
bombing took place. Target was clear, a wood to the north being
identified.'

On the night of 5/6 June 1944 15 Squadron sent 20 aircraft to
attack the coastal defences at Ouistreham as their contribution to
over 1,000 aircraft covering the invasion of Normandy. At dawn
they attacked a coastal battery that had been marked by the
Pathfinders, Brooks' crew noting, 'Some markers were seen 300
yards out to sea, with bombs falling on them. Cloud was 6/10 over
target area, and bombs were released after a timed run by instruments on red TIs.' 15 Squadron dropped 219 1,000lb bombs and 59
500lb bombs and 622 Squadron, also from Mildenhall, dropped 161
1,000lb bombs and 40 500lb bombs. The group report recorded,

> The Group's main force of Lancasters were out in strength (107
> Lancasters) bombing at sunrise the Coastal Batteries at
> Ouistreham which guarded, although the gunners probably
> did not realise it at the time, part of our beachhead. There is
> every reason to suppose that this attack was successful as very
> little opposition came from the Battery when the assault proper
> started.

On their return flight to Mildenhall the crews were able to see the
vast armada of shipping for the invasion laid out beneath them and
finally realised the vast scale of the operation of which they were a
tiny part. One 15 Squadron crew member noted in his log book, '"D"
Day Morning. Wonderful sight.'

On the night of 6/7 June the target was the railway at Lisieux on
one of the main German reinforcement routes to Normandy. The
railway was damaged but, unfortunately, the town itself was also
hit. On 10 June the crew dropped mines off the German coast and
on the 12th were back over Germany bombing the synthetic oil plant
at Gelsenkirchen. The crew reported, 'Bombing appeared accurate,
one large explosion being seen and considerable smoke.' The raid

Squadron Leader Pat Carden, who was Vic's pilot for his final few raids.
(Courtesy of Martyn Ford-Jones)

was such a success that oil production, of over 1,000 tons of fuel a day, was lost for several weeks.

On 21 June there was a daylight raid on a flying bomb base at Domleger, 15 miles east of Abbeville. The whole operation was a total failure, with 10/10 cloud blanketing the target. No target indicators could be seen and the Master Bomber cancelled the raid while the aircraft were over the target, forcing them to return home with a full bomb load. This was the final operational mission of Oliver Brooks who was granted leave and eventually became a flying instructor. Vic still had six missions left to fly of his standard thirty and, after leave himself, was assigned as Mid Upper Gunner to the crew of Acting Squadron Leader Pat Carden.

In July, 3 Group continued to attack launch sites and facilities for the German V Weapons, noting,

Just over 25% of our month's effort has been directed by day and night against the launching sites and depots of the flying bombs . . . Although it is difficult to assess the results of our work, it is plain that these continuous attacks by Allied aircraft are restricting the number of casualties and amount of damage in London and Southern England . . . Some of these targets have been attacked flying in formation line astern on a Pathfinder Oboe Mosquito Leader or on GH Stirlings of this Group, aircraft releasing on seeing the man in front release his bombs . . . Our formation flying, however, has not yet been 'buttoned up' and the pattern of bombs from other aircraft leaves much to be desired. Squadrons will have to get in what practice they can in flying in formation, whenever the spate of operations permits.

On 9 July the squadron bombed a flying bomb emplacement at Linzieux, but the crews did not claim any hits. Next day, thirteen aircraft were detailed for operations against a flying bomb storage depot at Nucourt, taking off in the early hours of the morning and bombing by instruments through 10/10 cloud. On the 18th the railway junction at Aulnoye was the target; twelve aircraft attacked, reporting accurate bombing, though haze and smoke over the target area made it hard to visually identify any ground detail. On the 20th they were back over Germany bombing synthetic oil plants at Homberg. The squadron résumé says, 'Reports indicate a successful raid, several large explosions being seen and huge fires that produced dense clouds of smoke. Enemy aircraft were very active and several combats were reported.' The crew report confirmed, 'At 01.20 hours a large orange explosion was seen, which on leaving was producing a plume of yellowish brown smoke up to 10,000 ft.' The ground explosions obviously impressed the Intelligence Officer who compiled the 3 Group report as it also commented, 'the raid was very successful and crews were rewarded by seeing an enormous explosion which belched out thick black smoke to a height of 14,000 feet'

On 5 August the attack was against oil-storage facilities at Bassens near Bordeaux with excellent results, the crew noting, 'Saw many fires & small explosions with black smoke above 4000'. M/B said "Bomb left of smoke for some undamaged buildings".' On the night of 7/8 August the target was a concentration of German forces at Rocque-Court in Normandy. For the first time in a while the squadron faced German night fighters and attacks were made on a number of aircraft, with that of Flight Lieutenant John Ball being lost with its entire crew. Carden's crew appear not to have noticed these attacks, reporting only that, 'Bombed to port side of Red TIs of M/B instructions. Bombing very concentrated. M/B very good.'

Vic's final raid (his thirty-first, one more than the standard thirty for a tour) was against a German oil-storage depot at Forêt De Lucheaux. There was no opposition from fighters and the target was well bombed, the crew noting, 'Green TI bombed was in centre of fires, smoke & Red TI as we bombed M/B instructed force to bomb fires which were burning nicely & spreading in different points of wood. Bombing concentrated.'

Having completed his tour and amassed a total of 402 flying hours, 152 of them on operations, Vic was attached briefly to 1657 Conversion Unit before being sent to the Aircrew Allocation Centre at RAF Brackla in Scotland. This was a holding unit designed to keep the men occupied and out of mischief while it was decided what to do with them. The centre had its own cinema and there were regular shows put on both by the camp residents themselves and by ENSA. Over the Christmas period, which was proclaimed a great success, the centre held an officers' mess dance, an all-ranks dance, a station concert party and a WAAF invitation dance, as well as community singing, comic soccer matches, children's parties and a free cinema show. The officers served the airmen's Christmas meal and there was an exchange of hospitality between the officers' and sergeants' messes. Every effort seems to have been made to make Christmas enjoyable.

While at Brackla, on 17 November 1944 Vic was awarded the Distinguished Flying Cross. The citation was included with four other RAAF warrant officers and reads: 'These officers have completed in various capacities, numerous operations against the enemy, in the course of which they have invariably displayed the utmost fortitude, courage and devotion to duty.'

On 19 January 1945 Vic returned to 11 PDRC outside Brighton pending his return to Australia. As with RAF Brackla, this was essentially a holding establishment; most of the men were put up in requisitioned hotels in the area. The weather in January 1945 was

Sergeant Vic Reid (left) with his colleague rear gunner Sergeant Eddie Oliver. (Courtesy of Martyn Ford-Jones)

abnormally severe and curtailed the usual range of sports available, with only three rugby and four hockey matches played, though most of the soccer games did go ahead. Indoor PT, squash and badminton proved popular, as did darts, cribbage and table tennis.

On 21 October 1944 Vic married Alice Catherine Rampling of 26 Stafford Road, Leytonstone. She was a year older than Victor, worked as a bus conductress and had lived in East London all her life. The marriage was just a few days before Vic's posting to Brackla, suggesting they'd met while he was with 15 Squadron, presumably while he was on leave in London.

Though information on what he did following his return to Australia is sparse, it doesn't seem to have been a happy period. He was transferred to the RAAF Reserve on 30 October 1945. There's no record I can trace of a divorce and his niece, Margaret Gregory, seems to think that he may have taken to drinking too much. Margaret told me, 'Victor got rotten drunk and drove his Jeep/Ute into the side of a bridge. One will never know if it was suicide as he had been depressed and drinking more than he should have for months before.' He died on 12 April 1951, aged 36 years. There's no record that Alice went to Australia with him and she seems to have remarried not long after his death.

Researching Vic Reid

I carried out research on Vic for his niece, Margaret, a few years ago, mainly filling in on the research she had already done in Australia. Australian rules on data protection are rather different from British ones and, because Margaret had requested his file be opened for her, the whole file is now available, online, for everyone to look at at no cost. It can be accessed at http://recordsearch.naa.gov.au/scripts/Imagine.asp?B=5534560.

A good place to start for Australian service records is the Australian World War 2 Nominal Roll, at http://www.ww2roll.gov.au, which gives very basic details of over 1 million Australian servicemen and women. You can search for service-record details by specifying any one of name, service number, honours, place (of birth, of enlistment or residential locality at enlistment). Once you find an individual service record you can print a certificate, which provides very basic details of their service, including place and date of enlistment, their service (air force, army or navy), service number, next of kin, rank, any honours or gallantry awards won and place of discharge. What you won't get are details of their postings and individual units served. The certificate for Victor provides the following basic information:

REID, VICTOR CHARLES

Service	Royal Australian Air Force
Service Number	421864
Date of Birth	7 Dec 1914
Place of Birth	TRIAMBLE, NSW
Date of Enlistment	28 Mar 1942
Locality on Enlistment	Unknown
Place of Enlistment	SYDNEY, NSW
Next of Kin	REID, ROBERT
Date of Discharge	2 Apr 1947
Rank	Warrant Officer
Posting at Discharge	AIR ARMAMENT AND GAS SCHOOL
WW2 Honours and Gallantry	Distinguished Flying Cross
Prisoner of War	No

The National Archives of Australia (http://www.naa.gov.au/index.aspx) hold Second World War service records and it's possible to request a copy of the full service record which can be viewed online or posted to you as a hard copy, at a cost. Under the Australian Archives Act (1983) the archives are required to provide as much information as possible, though separate medical files are not generally released.

Consisting of forty-eight pages (some are just file covers and many are parts of larger sheets photographed close up), Vic's file includes his Record of Service – Airmen (RAAF P/P.25) Form giving basic personal details, promotions, decorations, awards and badges, postings and attachments, movements and courses of instruction. If he'd been a casualty, committed a criminal offence or taken any exams towards promotion they would also be listed, though in Vic's case they don't apply. It has to be said that whoever photographed Vic's file certainly did a good job of it.

There's a link directly to the relevant pages of the National Archives of Australia website from the Australian World War 2 Nominal Roll website. The archive also has an extensive series of

fact sheets on the Second World War at http://www.naa
.gov.au/about-us/publications/fact-sheets/on-
defence/index.aspx#section4.

Though I prefer researching paper records where I can, I have to
admit that, as well as using the online version of Vic's service record
(Margaret had sent me a hard copy), I did use the Internet to locate
information on the RAAF in Australia, in particular http://www
.ozatwar.com/raaf/raaf.htm, a website devoted to the RAAF in the
Second World War, which was most useful.

Squadron and Group Records

Squadron records in AIR 27 series are now available online at TNA's
website (look in the RAF section of the Discovery section). In Vic's
case there is a slight complication – the compiler occasionally gets
his initial wrong and he appears as F/S E Reid and F/S U Reid
(though always with his RAAF number 421502, which makes things
easier) and later in the year there is a F/S F Reid who also served as
a gunner. Having said this, it's relatively easy, if you know the dates
he was posted to and from the squadron, to identify the raids he
took part in and read the crew's comments. The squadron also
provided a résumé of each raid to give a broader perspective. Every
squadron was part of a larger group (in 15 Squadron's case it was
No. 3 Group) and group ORBs are in AIR 25 series; in Vic's case the
relevant files covering 1944 are in AIR 25/53 with Appendices
(which frequently contain copies of the Group Monthly Summary)
in AIR 25/71 to AIR 25/80. An even broader perspective can be
gained from looking at these.

Combat Reports

As with fighter combat reports, those from Bomber Command are in
TNA's AIR 50 series, though the collection is known to be incomplete. They're available online through TNA's Discovery facility
and are searchable using surname and the squadron number.

The Squadron History

Sometimes there is nothing like a piece of good luck when carrying
out any kind of research. I've known Martyn Ford-Jones for over

twenty years, though it has to be said I hadn't seen him for quite a while when I bumped into him in the street. In the course of our conversation he mentioned, in passing, that he'd been appointed Official Historian for 15 Squadron! Not only that, he and his wife had written the Squadron History, *Oxford's Own – Men and Machines of 15/XV Squadron Royal Flying Corps/Royal Air Force* (Schiffer Military History, 1999; ISBN 0764309544). It's packed with facts, fascinating stories and rare photographs. Martyn kindly provided the photos that illustrate this chapter and a couple of stories are taken from his book or his huge archive of material on the squadron. It's worth bearing in mind that many excellent histories such as this are available and can save an enormous amount of original research.

The Bomber Command War Diaries – An Operational Reference Book 1939–1945, by Martin Middlebrook and Chris Everitt (Penguin Books, 1985), is an invaluable source for information on every raid carried out by the Command during the war.

Chapter 8

A GALLANT PATHFINDER CREW

One Pathfinder crew that achieved an incredible total of seventy-seven raids was piloted by Bill Cleland. Originally formed as a crew with 12 Squadron, it flew eleven missions with the squadron before it transferred to the Pathfinder Force, flying with 156 Squadron on operations until March 1945.

Having individually completed their training, the crew met up at RAF Faldingworth in Lincolnshire, where 1667 Heavy Conversion

Bill Cleland (centre) with his crew and ground crew at the end of their second tour of operations. (Courtesy of Jack Watson)

Unit took men who were used to twin-engined aircraft and trained them for the four-engined bombers. Sergeant Jack Watson, who'd recently completed his training as a flight engineer, was put into a hangar full of aircrew of all trades. He recalls,

> Suddenly a Wireless Operator came up to me and asked 'What's your name?' – 'John' I replied, 'Right Jack, we are looking for a Flight Engineer for our crew'. I was taken to meet the rest of the crew, where they had just found a Mid-Upper Gunner and so our crew was complete. That was how the Air Force let crew themselves decide who would fly with who. Needless to say I was Jack from then on, it was 1st November 1943.

The pilot was Flight Sergeant (later Flight Lieutenant) Bill Cleland, a university student at St Andrews who'd been in the University Air Squadron, been called up while still studying and learned to fly in the USA. Fond of quoting Shakespeare, he was more than just a pilot, as Jack describes, 'When he got into his seat it was as though he became the final part of the jigsaw puzzle that was an Avro Lancaster. It was like putting a printed circuit board into a piece of electronic equipment.'

The navigator was Gilbert Hudson, a serious man from Birmingham whose navigator's skills must have helped their selection for the Pathfinders. The bomb aimer was Frank Oliver from Hull; the wireless operator was Albert (Bert) Wilson from North Shields and another Geordie, Weston Appleby, was mid upper gunner. Their rear gunner left after a few days when he realised the difficulties of escaping from his turret in an emergency, and was replaced by Cliff Talbot. Bill gave each of them a nickname and this was what they used in the air. Jack became 'Watty', the navigator was 'Gilly', Appleby became 'Appy', Cliff Talbot was always Cliff, the radio operator was 'Willy' and the bomb aimer became 'Olly'.

They trained together for two months and, on 6 January 1944 were posted to 12 Squadron at RAF Wickenby. Jack describes the living accommodation,

> We were allocated a Nissen Hut and, as we were all Sergeants, we were all in the one hut. All the beds were just as the occu-

Bill Cleland's crew. Left to right: Willy, Mac, Gilly, Bill, Olly, Watty and Jack.
(Courtesy of Jack Watson)

pants had got out of them, the bed I put my kit on had the name over the bed, it read Sergeant Twitchet, he was the pilot of the crew who had occupied the hut . . . we discovered that Sgt Twitchet and his crew had not returned from the previous night's operations.

On 14 January they were briefed for their first raid, against the German city of Brunswick. Against a backdrop of a map of Europe with the route indicated by a red ribbon the commanding officer explained the purpose and method of the raid. The aircraft flew in a stream a few miles wide, affording each other some protection and would approach the target in waves to minimise collisions. The engineer leader detailed bomb and fuel loads, the gunnery leader detailed known gun and fighter areas and the navigator leader briefed on the finer points of the route. Everything was timed to the second, the navigators being issued with absolutely accurate watches that they had to hand back after every mission.

Their route took them over the North Sea to the Dutch coast, with Gilly telling Bill when to make the pre-planned turns and Jack monitoring fuel consumption. They reached the target exactly on time and Olly dropped their bombs to the right of the target indicators laid by the Pathfinders before returning to base without incident.

The squadron were part of No. 1 Group and the group report on the raid says:

> There was 10/10ths cloud in the target area, which prevented the majority of crews using the PFF ground markers and a large proportion of bombing was carried out on the emergency blind-bombing technique. The marking was scattered and somewhat spasmodic at the commencement but later built up to a fair concentration. The cloud prevented satisfactory observation of results but judged from the glow beneath the cloud the attack would appear to have been somewhat scattered with a tendency to spread towards the South, and no really satisfactory concentration appears to have been achieved. Whilst the ground defences in the target area were not impressive fighters were active.

Their second raid was to be against Berlin but Jack identified an engine problem so they turned aside and bombed Schwerin before returning home. Their next five raids included three against Berlin which Jack noted made all crews apprehensive because of the distance, and guns and searchlights that seemed to go on forever,

> There was always a Master Searchlight which was easily identifiable because it was a blue colour. As soon as it caught a plane in its beam a dozen more would converge on the plane it was holding. Then, only the quick reaction of the pilot could save the day as the anti-aircraft guns were also linked to the searchlights.

Being caught in the lights like this was known as being 'coned'.

On 20 February, on their eighth raid, against Stuttgart, they were attacked by a night fighter, Jack remembers, 'We had arrived over the target and just commenced the bombing run when we heard Appy call "Dive port go". Bill immediately put the aircraft into a corkscrew and I watched as the tracers from the fighter passed over the top of us. Appy's brilliant awareness and Bill's quick reaction had saved our lives.' Jack told me, using a much later phrase, that Appy had 'bionic eyes' and that his watchfulness saved them on more than one occasion.

After two months with 12 Squadron the crew were called to the Flight Commander's office and told, 'You have two options, either you volunteer for the Pathfinder Force or we will send you.' A Wing Commander from Pathfinder HQ had gone through the squadron records and selected them as one of the best crews. It was explained that, as Pathfinders, they would do two straight tours, totalling forty-five missions, five less than normal crews would do in their two tours. As a man, they volunteered to go.

They underwent a couple of weeks' intensive training, at RAF Warboys near Huntingdon, with the Pathfinder Navigational Training Unit. The bomb aimer now became navigator 2 and sat with navigator 1, assisting with some of the equipment. Jack, as flight engineer, assumed the bomb aimer's duties in addition to his own and was also trained to fly the aircraft if the pilot was hit. He recalls,

> This part I was more than happy to do, and I spent hours in the Link Trainer, which was a small flight simulator, and did for us what the sophisticated models do for today's airmen. It was a very basic model though and it was sufficient, as after a few hours I was able to put into practice, flying the Lancaster when on training flights. The Lancaster was a beautiful aircraft and a joy to fly.

Jack also had to train as bomb aimer by dropping small bombs at a target from 2,000ft and the whole crew had to train how to navigate.

They were now posted to 156 Squadron; an instructor told Jack they were known as a rebel squadron and that, as Jack recalls, 'they will fly till the cows come home and are the best, but there is not much discipline on the ground – they do not like a lot of bull'.

Pathfinders used an increasingly sophisticated range of navigational aids including H2S a ground-facing radar enabling them to locate rivers, lakes and built-up areas and Oboe, where signals from two stations in Britain were used to give the aircraft an accurate fix on its position. Targets were marked by one of three (or sometimes a combination) main methods. '*Paramatta*' used navigation aids to locate and mark the target; '*Newhaven*' used flares to illuminate the target so that Pathfinder aircraft could drop their target indicators on it; and *'Wanganui'* where the target was obscured by cloud and target indicators were dropped above it on parachutes, giving an aiming point for the following crews (also known as Sky Marking).

Their first raid was against Essen where they flew in support of the Master Bomber dropping flares to help him identify the target (and to draw some of the anti-aircraft fire).

Their second target was Nuremberg, on the night Bomber Command suffered its heaviest losses. The crew report for the raid, on the night of 30/31 March 1944 reads, 'Task. NURNBURG. Target attacked at 0106 hrs from 19,000 ft. Wanganui seen after leaving target area. No other observation owing to cloud conditions. H/H intense inaccurate. No S/L's. Fighter activity intense from south of RUHR to NURNBURG. One photo attempted.' Jack later recalled the raid,

Our second trip from Upwood, our thirteenth so far, was on the infamous Nuremberg raid in which 96 aircraft were lost. We were right in the front of the bomber stream, as we were to arrive first with the Marker Aircraft, as Supporters. We dropped our illuminating flares and then went round again for me, as Bomb Aimer, to drop our high explosives. Although we saw lots of activity, we had no trouble at all and we were never attacked. Being a bright moonlight night and with most aircraft leaving condensation trails and a route with long straight legs, in one case nearly 200 miles, it made life easy for the German fighters ... As we were on the last leg of the run into the target, Bert had reported he had picked up a blip on his Fishpond screen and from the way it was tracking us, he thought it was a fighter, unfortunately when a fighter got within a certain distance of us, it would disappear from the screen; it was when Appy noticed another Lancaster drifting across underneath us, that it blew up. Appy thought that the fighter was firing at us, but the other Lancaster was unlucky enough to have got in the way.

In the third week of April they flew five operations in seven days against Cologne, Düsseldorf, Karlsruhe, Essen and Freidrichs-haven. Over Düsseldorf Bill's skill saved them when, as Jack recalls,

As we started the bombing run I was getting ready to line up the bomb site when we were coned, Bill never hesitated and went into a dive, this forced me up to the front turret where I could not move. We had dived from eighteen thousand feet when Bill pulled up the nose at six thousand feet, this immediately threw me down onto the bomb sight. We still had to take evasive action until Bill managed to get out of the searchlights and it was only then that I was able to sort myself out. Finally I was able to get down to directing the bomb run and we bombed the target at twelve thousand feet. Getting coned in the searchlights is one of the most frightening things, as it feels as if you are standing on a stage absolutely naked. What must not happen, is for the crew to panic as only the pilot can deal with the situation . . . we all had great faith in Bill and he coped as we knew he would.

The squadron ORB confirms some of Jack's memories and provides lots of technical details, but omits the human drama. It says,

> Task: DUSSELDORF. Target attacked at 0116.00 hrs from 12,000 ft. At 0113 hrs first TI red seen falling. These formed a good concentration and were backed up by TI green. As we left target the bombing seemed well concentrated round markers but with a number of stragglers undershooting – some badly. Fires were burning well. Moderate to intense H/F, mostly barrage type, predicted and accurate for height. Numerous S/L's in many cones with 15/30 beams in each. One photo attempted. Bomb load 6 x 2,000 HC.

In May 1944 targets in France began to be attacked in preparation for D-Day. There were raids against rail junctions and an attack on the airfield at Nantes and on 5/6 June 156 Squadron bombed the German heavy coastal battery at Longues sur Mer, midway between what were to become Gold and Omaha beaches the next day. A week later, after bombing railways at Lens, the crew saw strange lights below them heading for Britain and only realised later these were the first V1s heading for London. Now they also started targeting V weapon stores and launch points, as well as concentrations of German troops in Normandy. Jack recalls,

> Early in August we did three trips near Paris to bomb the V1 (flying bomb) dumps. One of these trips was to Trossy, it was

heavily defended by anti aircraft guns and as we went in there was a huge bang and the aircraft went into a dive. I was in the nose and had just dropped the bombs when I looked through the Perspex dome which allowed me to look under the aircraft, I could see the propellors were all still turning okay, so I went up to make sure Bill was okay and he was. We got away with damage to the bomb doors and an engine casing.

After the third raid there was an incident on the ground when an accidental explosion killed two gunners from other crews. An off the cuff remark to Cliff Talbot seems to have made him think about his own fate. Jack wrote, 'We could only assume he had decided to stop flying, as nobody could or would tell us where he had gone.' He was replaced by a 19-year-old Canadian, John MacGregor, who stayed with them until their final operational mission.

In the middle of October they finished their second tour, which had been increased by five missions because French raids were not considered to be as dangerous as raids over Germany (though as Jack points out, 'Aircraft still got shot down . . . and the crews that did not come back were just as dead'). Nevertheless, Bill tried to persuade them to sign on for another tour and knowing that he was going to anyway, the rest of the crew elected to stay with him.

In late December 1944 the German offensive began in the Ardennes and Bomber Command switched to bombing the marshalling yards being used to bring reinforcements to the front. An attack on the railway yards at Cologne on 30 December was reported by 8 Group:

> Both TIs and skymarkers were used in difficult cloud conditions. Marking was good and sustained throughout the attack, although in the latter stages there was a tendency for it to become scattered. Again assessment of results was difficult although reports from the more experienced crews indicate that the area between the Marshalling Yard and the river suffered. Several large explosions were observed.

With Luftwaffe opposition becoming less frequent some daylight operations were now carried out over Germany itself. Jack describes a raid,

In January 1945 we went on a daylight raid to Saarbrucken. We had a fighter escort of American Mustang fighters and after we had finished our bombing run we turned for home, I checked to make sure all the bombs had gone; one 1000lb bomb had hung up and not released. When I told Bill he said we would go back and try again. We were about 50 miles from the target by now, as we turned one of the Mustangs turned with us and escorted us back to Saarbrucken. We made two runs, but did not succeed in releasing the bomb, so we turned for home. Over the sea on the way back we tried again but still with no success. When we got back Bill called up the control tower and told them of our predicament and we were given permission to land. As we came in, when Bill put full flap, the bomb suddenly shot forward and landed on the bomb doors. We landed okay but as we taxied our way back to dispersal the bomb doors were being strained by the weight on them. When we stopped at dispersal the normal procedure was to open the bomb doors; not this time though. Five months previously, when an aircraft was being unloaded, when the bombs had been brought back, they had exploded killing six of the ground staff. With this in mind we got out of the aircraft as quickly as we could, this time, the armourers were able to deal with the bomb quite successfully.

At the end of their third tour Bill again persuaded them to continue flying. They were now so experienced that at Cologne (2 March) and Harpenerweg (24 March) they were Deputy Master Bomber. The Cologne raid was the last the RAF made on the city, the Pathfinders marked in clear weather and a carpet of high explosives was laid over the city. On 25 March they were Master Bomber for a raid of 175 aircraft against the railway route through Munster.

On their return from the Munster raid the crew were told by a friend from another crew that a signal had come through ordering them off operations immediately; they'd just completed their seventy-seventh mission. Three weeks later they were broken up as a crew; Bill was seconded to BOAC (and stayed with them and later British Airways until he retired); Bert ended up, still flying, in Iraq. Jack was posted to 85 Operational Training Unit at Husbands Bosworth in Leicestershire, where he tried to get back into operational flying, and was told off for doing so.

What Made Such a Successful Crew?

Having spoken to both Jack and Bill, read Jack's memoir and log book and gone through every report they submitted, it's clear Bill's crew was highly professional, but was there something more? There's no doubt that Bill, as a brilliant pilot, was the crew's bedrock and they were incredibly loyal to him, even agreeing to continue flying missions at his request when not required to. When Bill was a child his father died, leaving his mother to cope with him and his younger brother and sister; perhaps this early responsibility, having to assist her in looking after his younger siblings, helped him develop his sense and air of responsibility.

Jack tells me that he only once heard Bill raise his voice when, during a raid, one of the new navigators came forward and commented in amazement at the flak that they were flying through. Bill shouted, 'Get back', which was instantly obeyed. Otherwise, he never raised his voice and he remained softly spoken to his death. The same navigators, having newly joined the crew, made mistakes on their first two missions taking the aircraft dangerously off course. The rest of the crew had a word with Bill and he, in turn, spoke to the navigators. Quite what was said to them Jack doesn't know – but afterwards their navigation greatly improved.

Though Bill, as pilot, was in command of the aircraft, he didn't stand on ceremony. When Appy called down, 'Bill, Dive Left', Bill

Jack Watson (right) with Appy (left), Eddy (from another crew, second left) and Bert.
(Courtesy of Jack Watson)

ROYAL AIR FORCE

PATH FINDER FORCE

Award of
Path Finder Force Badge

Jack Watson's Path
Finder Force Badge
certificate.
(Courtesy of Jack
Watson)

𝕿𝖍𝖎𝖘 𝖎𝖘 𝖙𝖔 𝖈𝖊𝖗𝖙𝖎𝖋𝖞 that

1805406

FLIGHT SERGEANT WATSON. J. R. D.F.M.

having qualified for the award of the Path Finder Force Badge, and

having now completed satisfactorily the requisite conditions of

operational duty in the Path Finder Force, is hereby

Permanently awarded the Path Finder Force Badge

Issued this **7th** day of **APRIL** in the year 19**45**

Air Officer Commanding, Path Finder Force.

dived, no questions asked – this willingness to trust his crew implicitly saved them on more than one occasion. He also trusted Jack's judgment about the state of the aircraft, pressing on with missions when assured that problems with the aircraft would not prejudice their chances of success.

Crew Medal Citations and Recommendations

Bill Cleland's DFC recommendation reads,

Pilot Officer Cleland has completed 30 operational sorties, 19 of which have been with the Pathfinder Force. The targets attacked have included some of the most heavily defended in

Germany. This officer is an exceptionally determined and skilful Captain and Pilot, and beneath his quiet and unassuming manner is a dogged determination to achieve his objective regardless of enemy opposition. He has produced consistently good results, and is fearless in pressing home his attacks. I recommend him for the award of the Distinguished Flying Cross.

The recommendation for Bill's DSO reads,

Acting Flight Lieutenant William John CLELAND, DFC (174404) Royal Air Force Volunteer Reserve, No 156 Squadron. (Pilot/Captain of aircraft; sorties 73; flying hours 363; since previous award, sorties 43; flying hours 201.) This officer has always displayed a fine fighting spirit and great zest for operations. He has a fine record of operational sorties and has always shown outstanding courage and determination, even in the face of heaviest opposition. Many of his missions have entailed the fulfilment of difficult and dangerous duties. He has invariably performed them with great gallantry and efficiency. Flight Lieutenant Cleland has always set a high standard of tenacity and devotion to duty.

Jack Watson's recommendation for his DFM says,

Flight Sergeant Watson has now completed 55 operational sorties, 44 of which have been with the Path Finder Force. Many of his targets have been heavily defended German areas.

    This N.C.O. is a keen and efficient Flight Engineer who has shown courage and resourcefulness on many perilous operations. His aircraft has many times been attacked and damaged by enemy action, but Flight Sergeant Watson has always risen to the occasion and given valuable assistance to his Captain.

    He has shown zest and devotion to duty of the highest order, and I recommend him for the award of the Distinguished Flying Medal.

For Gilbert Hudson the recommendation says (after giving details of the raids he'd been on),

This Officer is an accurate and reliable Navigator, and has shown the utmost determination and courage in carrying out his duties under extremely difficult conditions. He has always shown great keenness in his operational career, and has always been willing to assist in his section. His loyalty and devotion to duty have been of a high order, and I recommend him for the Distinguished Flying Cross.

For Flight Sergeant Weston Appleby it reads,

This NCO, by his vigilance and correct directions to his pilot, has on many occasions been responsible for the successful evasion of enemy aircraft. He is a courageous and determined gunner and is unflinching in the face of enemy attacks. He has been involved in many hazardous operations, but in spite of which his operational zest is still undiminished.

His devotion to duty has been of a high order, and I recommend him for the award of the Distinguished Flying Medal.

For Flight Sergeant Albert John Charles Wilson the commendation says,

This NCO is a keen and determined Wireless Operator, and has proved himself to be an able and reliable member of a good Blind Marking crew in the squadron. He has always carried on with his work coolly and efficiently under adverse conditions, and his results have been of a high standard.

His devotion to duty has at all times been of a high order, and I recommend him for the award of the Distinguished Flying Medal.

For Pilot Officer James Allistair MacGregor it reads:

This officer is a cool and determined Gunner who is unflinching in the face of enemy opposition. He has plenty of grit and tenacity, and possesses a fine zest for operational work. He is an asset to any crew.

Pilot Officer MacGregor has shown a high standard of keenness, loyalty and devotion to duty, and I recommend him for the award of the Distinguished Flying Cross.

For Pilot Officer Frank Oliver it says:

This Officer is a most efficient and reliable Set Operator of special equipment who has always produced good results. His skill and determination is reflected in the success of a good Blind Marking crew with whom he operates.

He has set a fine example of devotion to duty, and I recommend him for award of the Distinguished Flying Cross.

Combat Operations as Taken from Jack Watson's Log Book

12 Squadron, RAF Wickerby

14/01/1944	Brunswick	
20/01/1944	Berlin	(Bombed L.R. Schwerin, Returned to Base on 3 engines)
21/01/1944	Magdeburg	
27/01/1944	Berlin	
28/01/1944	Berlin	(Landed at Ludford Magna)
30/01/1944	Berlin	
19/02/1944	Leipzig	
20/02/1944	Stuttgart	(Attacked by fighters over target)
24/02/1944	Schweinfurt	
25/02/1944	Augsberg	
01/03/1944	Stuttgart	

156 Squadron, PFF Upwood

26/03/1944	Essen	
30/03/1944	Nuremburg	(Landed away at Marham)
20/04/1944	Cologne	
22/04/1944	Düsseldorf	(Coned Bombed at 12,000)
24/04/1944	Karlsruhe	
26/04/1944	Essen	(Coned)
27/04/1944	Freidrichshafen	

30/04/1944	Somain	(France)
03/05/1944	Montdidier	(France)
07/05/1944	Nantes	(France) 5 Bombing runs
19/05/1944	Boulogne Area	RDF Station
21/05/1944	Duisburg	
22/05/1944	Dortmund	
24/05/1944	Aachen	
03/06/1944	Calais	(Coastal batteries)
05/06/1944	Longues	(Coastal battery 'D' Day)
07/06/1944	Foret-de-Ceresy	(Ammo dump)
08/06/1944	Fougres	(Marshalling yards bombed from 4,000 feet)
15/06/1944	Lens	(Marshalling yards)
17/06/1944	Montdidier	Illum. (Brought bombs back)
24/06/1944	Middelstraete	(Flying bomb launch area)
27/06/1944	Oisemont-Neuville	(Landed away at Woodbridge)
02/07/1944	Oisemont-Neuville	
23/07/1944	Donges	(Oil stores) Illum.
24/07/1944	Stuttgart	(End of 1st tour of operations)
25/07/1944	Stuttgart	(Flares brought back bombed visually)
28/07/1944	Hamburg	(T.I.'s & sky marking P.B.M.)
03/08/1944	Cassan N.W. Paris	(Flying bomb dumps)
04/08/1944	Trossy	(Fly bomb dumps holed by flak)
05/08/1944	Construction works nr Abbeville	
07/08/1944	Battle area S. Caen	
09/08/1944	Petrol Dump nr Lille	
12/08/1944	Russelheim nr Frankfurt	Buzz Bomb construction works. B Illum. Bombs dropped on second run. Holed by flak over target. Attacked by fighters.
16/08/1944	Kiel.	P.B. Illum.
18/08/1944	Connantre	P.B. Illum.

25/08/1944	Russelheim nr Frankfurt.	P.B. Illum.
26/08/1944	Kiel.	P.B. Illum.
12/09/1944	Frankfurt	(Illum. Bombed visually. Coned. Slight damage by flak).
15/09/1944	Kiel.	P.B. Illum.
16/09/1944	Moerdijk (Holland)	(Illum. Bombed visually on second run. Road bridge over estuary).
20/09/1944	Calais	(Bombed 3,000 ft on second run. Onzard trip. No flak).
05/10/1944	Saarbrucken	B.S.M.
14/10/1944	Duisburg	(Holed by flak. M/P Fuselage).

End of second tour of operations.

15/10/1944	Wilhelmshaven	
02/11/1944	Düsseldorf	(Took S/L Robertson's crew)
03/12/1944	Heimbach	URFT Dam.
12/12/1944	Essen	
17/12/1944	Duisburg	(U.B.U.)
28/12/1944	Opladen	(U.C.)
30/12/1944	Cologne	(U.C.)
02/01/1945	Nuremburg	(STB. Inner feathered owing to technical failure)
05/01/1945	Hannover	(U.C.)
14/01/1945	Saarbrucken	(U.C.)
16/01/1945	Magdeburg	(U.C.)
28/01/1945	Stuttgart	(Attacked by ME 410 over target. No damage to A/C).
01/02/1945	Mainz	(U.C.)
02/02/1945	Weisbaden	(U.C.)
08/02/1945	Politz nr Stettin	(U.C.)
13/02/1945	Bohlen nr Leipzig	(P.U.M.)

End of third tour of operations.

17/02/1945	Wesel	(U.C.) Bombs brought back on Master Bomber instructions owing to cloud.
21/02/1945	Worms	(U.C.)

02/03/1945	Cologne	Deputy Master Bomber. Over target 25 mins. Slight flak damage.
05/03/1945	Chemnitz	(P.U.M.)
18/03/1945	Hanau nr Frankfurt (P.U.M.)	
22/03/1945	Hildesheim nr Hanover (P.U.M.)	
24/03/1945	Harpenerweg nr Dortmund prang.	Deputy Master Bomber. Good
25/03/1945	Munster	Master Bomber.

Researching a Pathfinder Crew

Having copies of Jack's log book and short memoir was a great aid in getting started and provided much of the material in this chapter, greatly assisted by being able to speak with Jack himself and Bill Cleland.

One advantage to having a log book is it provides details of the many training and practice flights carried out in the course of normal duties (see Chapter 7, where, in the absence of a log, it's only possible to locate Vic Reid's operational sorties). In September 1944, for example, as well as three night raids and a daylight raid, Bill's crew carried out ten daylight flights testing equipment and practising air-to-air firing. It also pointed up an error in the squadron records – the log records a raid against Leipzig on 19 February 1944 – but the ORB contains no crew report. Only on checking the squadron résumé is it confirmed that the crew took part as Bill's name is mentioned as among the pilots participating. One should always remember – it's possible that even the best-kept official records may contain errors!

The ORB for 12 Squadron in early 1944 is in AIR 27/168, with Appendices in AIR 27/170 and AIR 27/171. The ORBs for 156 Squadron are in AIR 27/1042, 1043 and 1044. They're available for download (for a charge) via the Discovery section of TNA's website. It's interesting to note the wealth of technical detail in the 156 Squadron ORB regarding their equipment, the opposition and the general conduct of the raids.

For an overall picture of each raid, as seen from the perspective of 8 Group, the group ORBs are in AIR 25 series between AIR 25/161 and AIR 25/174, most of which consist of Appendices, including the group monthly summaries from which some of the detailed quotes about the raids are taken.

The RAF's own website at http://www.raf.mod.uk/bomber-command/background.html gives orders of battle, methods of locating targets and German fighter and other defences.

Crew Medal Recommendations

For details of their medal awards, which are scattered, un-indexed, throughout TNA's AIR 2 ('DECORATIONS, MEDALS, HONOURS AND AWARDS') series I was fortunate to know Paul Baillie, a veteran researcher who privately indexed the awards many years ago and who provides references for a small fee. He was quickly able to advise the initial references are:

Cleland: DSO AIR 2/9080; DFC AIR 2/9275
Hudson: DFC AIR 2/8826
Oliver: DFC AIR 2/9037
Wilson: DFM AIR 2/8880
Appleby: DFM AIR 2/8880
MacGregor: DFC AIR 2/9058.

These references refer only to the Master File (initial lists of recommendations) but each recommendation comes with an individual reference, i.e., the number of the recommendation either within the particular AIR 2 file or in the files immediately following. For Jack Watson, for example, the Master File reference is in AIR 2/8829 and the recommendation itself in AIR 2/8830.

An excellent website devoted to 156 Squadron at www .156squadron.com provides a potted history, maps, photographs of squadron members and aircraft, details of missions, crew lists, details from the ORBs, a roll of honour and links to related sites. It's one of those sites (and the RAF does seem to attract them) set up by an avid enthusiast with an eye for detail, a love of the subject and people and the patience and ability to set up a website.

Chapter 9

A WREN IN THE FLEET AIR ARM – JANET PEGDEN

The years following the Second World War were times of great change for the air services bringing reductions in scale and the change from propeller aircraft to jet engines. In the Fleet Air Arm the first jet aircraft were introduced in the late 1940s, though they were initially difficult to operate from aircraft carriers because of their size and weight. Gradual improvements in both the jets themselves and in aircraft carriers (including angled flight decks and steam catapults) meant that, during the 1950s, jets became the norm. Though as a woman she wasn't allowed to serve aboard a ship, Janet Pegden served with the FAA for ten years in the Women's Royal Naval Service (WRNS – or Wrens) as a mechanic and then a pilot's mate, responsible for the total maintenance of an aircraft. Still a sprightly 80-year-old living in Highworth, near Swindon, she clearly recalls her days as a Wren. I had the pleasure of sitting in on an interview she did for the IWM and to speaking and corresponding with her myself, then following up her description of an air crash to which she was a witness and finding the minutes of the Board of Enquiry to which she gave evidence.

Janet Pegden was born on 9 September 1931 at Ramsgate and for the first few years of her life lived with her parents and grandparents on a farm near Margate. She lived later at Stodmarsh near Canterbury after death duties and back payment of church tithes forced her father to give up her grandfather's farm. In 1938 the harsh winter forced her father to go to work for another farmer, then on to airfield construction work near Newark.

During the Battle of Britain she watched dog fights over Kent and remembers doing air-raid practice, running from school to hide under the pews in the local church. She watched oil tanks on the

137

coast being repeatedly bombed and a German land mine came down near her village. Her mum and dad did fire watching and her dad also served in the Home Guard.

Because she moved schools so frequently Janet could barely read before the age of 9. However, with the encouragement of her mother, who introduced her to the library at WH Smith, and the headmaster of the school at Elham, who kept his eye on her and forced her to work and concentrate, she caught up with her education. At the age of 13 she started at Folkestone County Technical School for Girls, which gave her a good all-round education, and stayed until she was 17½.

On leaving school Janet wanted to be a vet but was dissuaded by her father, who told her that 'no farmer would like to discuss his cow's internal arrangements with a young woman'. She then decided she'd like to be a physiotherapist but while she enjoyed the theory, she didn't like the practical side. Still not sure what she was going to do with herself, Janet went to see her aunt at Feltham, where a neighbour who'd been a WRNS officer said, 'There are all kinds of things you can do', so she sent away for the papers. Her father was dead against it because, as Janet explained, 'The women's services tended to be portrayed as good time girls – they weren't really – it was just the *Daily Mail*!' She initially considered applying to boats crews but was told that they were closing that part of the service down, so she applied to be a mechanic as she'd always enjoyed taking things to pieces and had acquired a good grasp of the basics through working with her father.

After receiving her acceptance papers Janet went up for her official medical in October or November 1949 and afterwards was sent to Burghfield – near Greenham Common – even though she hadn't actually officially signed on. Arriving by train, the group was met by an officer who directed the girls to a lorry to take them to the camp. On the lorry she met Felicity, another recruit who had joined against her parents' wishes' and with whom she shared a room. They were kitted out in awful stockings, long bloomers, sensible, flat shoes and a blue overall, with their hair done up in hideous turbans. Accommodation was in a barrack block with a shared room for two – ablutions were down the hall. The recruits were given a fortnight's basic training, marching around in horrible blue overalls with thick, black stockings. Very few girls had problems with marching – they were helped by music played over a

Janet Pegden's initial WRNS training course at Burghfield near Newbury. (Courtesy of Janet Boddy, née Pegden)

tannoy. They had classroom lessons in naval terms, they learned knots, naval ranks (and ranks in the other services) with instruction in what they might do in the service. The other recruits came from a variety of backgrounds and two surprised Janet and Felicity by coming back late one night roaring drunk. It was only after the fortnight that the WRNS were asked to sign on and some from the course decided not to do so. Having signed on, there followed another fortnight being taught how to look after their uniforms and more classroom lectures before the course split up to be posted to the next training establishment.

In Janet's case this was the Royal Naval Air Station at Yeovilton to do basic training as an air mechanic. Here she had lessons in theory, learnt oil systems, how to change filters, ignition systems (all you needed to learn was 'Suck, squash, bang, blow' to understand the sequence), how to time the engine to prevent backfires, how to keep the filters clean and how to use screwdrivers and spanners. She learnt the theory of flight, how to strip and rebuild a Tiger Moth engine then run it, how to handle aircraft, folding the wings, moving aircraft on the ground – where to push and where not to push – you couldn't push the pitot heads, for example, putting the chocks in, signalling the aircraft when moving on the ground, sometimes using illuminated wands at night. She was

139

given her own toolkit – ratchet screwdriver, spanners, lots of other screwdrivers, feeler gauges for checking spark-plug gaps, a hacksaw, box spanners, tommy bars, all in a wooden box 18in long, 14in wide and a foot high, painted in individual colours with the owner's name on it.

Accommodation comprised Nissen huts with about fifteen girls housed in each, with big, black stoves for warmth, wooden floors and wardrobes for kit. On a typical day at Yeovilton Janet was always awake early and used to sing on her way to the showers, then eat an enormous breakfast, then to the parade ground for inspection and sometimes a bit of PT – running and star jumps – then double-up or march to the classrooms or the hangar. There was stand easy when the NAAFI van came round. Lunch was at midday; with more training between 1pm and 4.30pm. Supper was at 6pm then quite often there were duties – in the regulating office checking people in or out or peeling potatoes. Food was plentiful but basic; if you were working late the cook would leave food – you could literally bounce the eggs like a rubber ball! Lots of baked beans, kidneys on fried bread, steak and kidney pudding or pie, fish and chips and lots of vegetables. If you worked late and entered the galley, on switching on the light you could see the floor was literally moving with cockroaches which would crush underfoot. Janet recalls,

The monthly Captain's Rounds [kit inspection] were nerve racking – you polished the floor until it was absolutely shiny, you'd clean and wash everything, shoes had to be polished, including the soles – a lot of us kept special shoes for inspections, the bed linen was all folded – the bedspread had to be on the right way round – with the anchor facing your feet, otherwise it would sink a sailor apparently. Everything had to be folded neatly. Your locker had to be spotless. You were allowed to have a couple of personal items like photographs on display. We'd all clear out and the Captain and his staff, the Chief Wren, the Regulating Officer etc. would have the place all to themselves. The Regulating Officer used to tear around first to check everything was all right. Lord Nuffield, who was a great philanthropist, had given a lot of money to the WRENs and some had been spent supplying sanitary towels – not that many were used for the purpose for which they were intended; they were usually used for polishing rags. One awful day the

Regulating Officer came round and found one plonk in the middle of the floor where it had been used for polishing. She snatched it up and ran off with it!

Janet also took her first flight,

My first flight was in a Dominee, which was our version of the De Haviland Rapide. We were on our last phase of training, and we had to go in uniform, complete with hat. There was nothing else for it, so I used my hat [to be sick into]! When we got in, I found the nearest outside drain and cold tap, turned my hat inside out, gave it a good wash, rung it out, put it on, and was fit to salute any officer around!

Janet was posted to Lossiemouth in June 1950 as an air mechanic (engines). She loved both the long railway journey there and the base itself, which was near to the sea so you could walk to the beach across the golf course. She worked mainly on the Fairey Firefly and was assigned to a ground crew consisting of the Chief, PO Engines and PO Airframes, a couple of leading hands and then the 'Erks'. A group of electricians, under a separate Chief, would also be assigned. First thing they were taught was how to drain the oil and how to clean and change the oil filters (using petrol to clean them). They were trained to remove the engine using an overhead crane, having carefully removed the engine seating bolts and all attachments for the controls, oil and hydraulics, after which it could be easily removed. A dozen or so Fireflies were all being worked on at once in the hangar, where all the major maintenance jobs were carried out. All components were changed after a certain number of flying hours. Janet remembers,

Folding the wings was fun – the hanger floor was very greasy – there's a little eyelet in the tip of the wing and you thread a rope through that and you have a gang of chaps on both ends of the rope and you all start pulling in the direction that it's folded and it goes right up– someone has to stand on the fuselage and pull out this leg that hooks into a socket and it can be quite unnerving to do this in case it went through the wrong place. The concrete floor was awfully greasy most of the time and used to sweat and we all wore rubber soled plimsolls and

141

when we got to the point where it was balanced you'd all have to swing round so that you were lowering it gently – but sometimes somebody would lose their balance and you'd all snake about on the floor trying to hold it steady. I used to enjoy the varied work, changing the plugs, starter changes – Coffman starters – you'd fill them with cartridges, rather like big shotgun cartridges – it was fired from the cockpit by an electrical charge and it would explode and start the engine. The engine had to be primed by pumping the choke; sometimes it wouldn't start and then you'd have to have another go. We looked after the Sea Otter flying boat, refuelling and starting up – this was done with a generator. It was very slow but very good for air sea rescue because it would land on the sea – except when it was very rough.

Janet Pegden (in overalls, standing, right) and fellow Wrens working on a Griffon engine at RNAS Eglinton – a photograph staged for the local newspaper. (Courtesy of Janet Boddy, née Pegden)

After two-and-a-half years Janet was posted to RNAS Culdrose but was only there for a month and then her leading wren's course came through so back she went to Yeovilton. The leading wren's course was 'the same as before only more so' with a lot of fitting, turning and lathe work, a lot more on the theory of flight – she also started training to work on jet aircraft. Janet was not a fan of jet engines; she tells me you had to check the turbine blades and refuel them but there wasn't as much to do on them.

After a six-month course she was posted to Eglinton near Londonderry with 737 Training Squadron,

> I loved it there – I liked the people and the life. I used to pedal across the airfield every day on a bike – it was very spread out. Accommodation was in big huts with about a dozen Wrens, all in one big room – as a Leading Wren I was supposed to be in charge. Leading Wrens had different duties; we were expected

Wren ground crew on the wing of a Fleet Air Arm Firefly at RNAS Eglinton. (Courtesy of Janet Boddy, née Pegden)

to give orders and be a little bit more responsible, but it didn't change my relationship with other Wrens.

We used to have courses of pilots coming through who'd do take-off and landing practices, gunnery and bomb dropping practice. We had to do daily inspections, checking oil levels and tyres, which were particularly important.

While at Eglinton Janet was sent to do a pilot's mate course. Pilots' mates were responsible for the whole aircraft, they uncovered it, checked the flaps, ailerons and rudder worked, made sure there was no damage at all, put the pilot's parachute in, then strapped him in and saw him off, helping to manoeuvre him on the ground using signals. There was a team of specialist armourers and electricians who repaired items of equipment identified as not working but responsibility for identifying faults lay with the mate. It was a fairly routine job, but, according to Janet, a fun one,

Janet Pegden (seated, second left) with the award-winning .22 rifle WRNS team at RNAS Eglinton. (Courtesy of Janet Boddy, née Pegden)

[At Eglinton] We used to do a bit of horse riding, played a bit of tennis and had dances. We used to have a grand Halloween Dance every year and I used to dress up as a witch. I was in the shooting team – we won a silver medal once. Target shooting and for .22 rifles small tiles you shoot off a ledge at 25 yards done within a time. .303 targets were a foot square but you'd fire at them up to a 1,000 yards. The Queen Mary Competition started at 1,000 yards and the target came closer, down to 200 yards, but by the time it was so close you were exhausted. We also had snap shooting when the chaps in the butts would hold the target up and drop it down again.

Janet almost got sent to Bisley, the home of British shooting and where only the best shots get to compete, and did win one or two little cups. She also took another memorable flight, 'I came over from Ireland with a flight to an airfield near Newark. (R.A.F.) I had to refuel, and give the plane a once over. Sick again. AND on the way back!'
On another flight,

I went up on a test flight and did rolls, looped the loop and stalls and everything. It was fun. I hung on to my breakfast

Fleet Air Arm servicing crew at RNAS Althorne. (Courtesy of Janet Boddy, née Pegden)

145

until we came into land. I well remember the pilot who took me up on the test flight. He was called De Malpas-Finlay. He had a terrible stutter, except when he was on the RT. He also wore very thick glasses, and un-nerved his passengers by asking them to direct him to the airfield!! Apparently, he was flying a helicopter in Singapore, and something happened and he went in. He was heard all over the ship BBBBugger!

Witness at a Board of Enquiry

While serving at RNAS Eglinton Janet witnessed the fatal crash of a FAA Firefly, No. T2 MB 566, piloted by Lieutenant T A Tallon, with Acting Sub-Lieutenant J E Brazenor as Observer. She was waiting for her own aircraft to come in when, in the distance, she saw the Firefly suddenly dive into Lough Foyle. Glancing up at the control tower, she assumed, from their reaction, that they'd also witnessed the accident, so she concentrated on getting her own pilot and aircraft safely into the shed before mentioning the incident to the CPO in charge. She was promptly turned about and marched directly to the tower to explain what she had seen; no one in the tower had seen anything and she was closely questioned before being dismissed. As one of the few people who had actually seen the start of the incident she was called to give evidence at the Board of Enquiry, which was held at Eglinton on 18 March 1954, ten days after the accident.

Q 65:   Will you tell us what you saw?

A: I was on No 737 Squadron Hard Standing on the 8th March 1954, about half past four. I was waiting for my aircraft and was looking out over 'B' and 'C' dispersals, just over towards the Foyle from where I was, and I saw the aircraft about 1" or 2" above the skyline and I saw it for about 2 seconds and then it suddenly put its nose down and as it did, it turned on its back and went in an absolutely vertical dive. I couldn't see it actually crash into the water because it disappeared behind the trees, but I saw nothing fall from the aircraft and there was no smoke; as far as I could see the undercarriage was retracted. That's about all I can say.

Q 66: How far would you say the aircraft was from you when you first saw it?

A: It is very difficult for me to say, but I could just tell it was a Firefly, but not what mark it was or it's number. I should say about 6 miles at least.

Q 67: How much nose down would you say the aircraft reached before starting to roll? What was the position and direction of the aircraft relative to you?

A: From where I was it was in line with 'B' and 'C' dispersals and above the skyline about 2". It was about across my line of vision but going away very slightly.

Q 68: Will you try to describe very carefully what you saw of the aircraft nosing down and rolling?

A: I first saw the aircraft across my line of vision for about 2 seconds, then the nose started to fall and the starboard wing dropped at the same time and it went over completely on to it's back and then went into a vertical dive.

Q 69: Did you get the impression that the aircraft continued to roll throughout is dive?

A: No, it looked to me as if it went straight and then turned over.

Q 70: Did it appear to go down vertically?

A: Yes, Sir.

Q 71: Then you lost sight of it?

A: Yes, the trees are quite high over there.

Q 72: Can you give any estimate as to how high the aircraft was before it went into its dive?

A: It is rather difficult to say. It must have been going down for 2 to 3 seconds and then I lost sight of it.

Janet answered some other questions regarding the weather, which had been sunny, confirmed that she had seen nothing fall from the aircraft and had seen no smoke. She confirmed that she'd been a Wren looking after aircraft for four years and three months and that she'd previously witnessed air crashes. Having given her evidence she withdrew and was not recalled.

Other witnesses gave evidence about the state of the aircraft, the nature of the flight (it was just a short one to test instruments) the weather and their view of the crash.

The Accident Report was issued on 23 June 1954 and was inconclusive, mainly because only part of the wreckage could be recovered from the Lough, but one point of concern was noted. The Firefly was a 'G Dropper', an aircraft fitted with G-type dinghy droppers mounted in bomb racks on the wings. Though Janet hadn't seen any smoke when the aircraft commenced its dive, other witnesses said they'd seen what appeared to be a puff of white smoke. Following the Board of Enquiry the wreckage was re-examined, concentrating on the torn-off starboard tail plane and elevator and the G-type droppers and also to one of the dinghies that had been found draped over the tail. Careful measurement of the parachute lines between the dinghy and container showed the total length of the lines and the dinghy would allow it to reach the tail-plane area and examination of the tail plane itself revealed two small marks and a tiny fragment of fibre closely resembling the buoyancy cord of the dinghy. There had been incidences of dinghies being prematurely released when aircraft were on the ground (one actually occurred at Eglinton, ten days after the accident Janet witnessed) but the Accident Report could only comment:

> Without the engine and remainder of the unrecovered wreckage it impossible to arrive at any positive opinions as to the cause of the accident. The evidence relating to the 'G' droppers is far too inconclusive to venture an opinion as to whether premature release of the dinghy took place. If a dinghy were to fall from its container, out of sequence, it is still problematic whether the result would be to foul the flap and set up an unstable condition, or whether the result would drogue back and upwards sufficiently to foul the elevator horn balance. It is known, however, that when the dinghy is inflated a small cloud of chalk is released which is visible to onlookers.

Even though the report was inconclusive, its one recommendation is telling, 'It is understood that an improved "G" Dropper container is being developed. If this is so then it is recommended that its production and issue to the Service be hastened as it is considered that the present container is extremely flimsy and, if not maintained in virtually 100% condition, could be extremely dangerous.'

Over the course of her ten years as a Wren in the FAA Janet worked mainly on Fireflies and Sea Furies, though she also worked on Ansons, Sea Otters, Gannets and Scimitars. While at Eglinton she even helped refuel three Spitfires of the Irish Air Force that landed there, though since they rarely overflew Northern Ireland airspace quite what they were doing these she isn't sure.

After her service at Eglinton, Janet attended a petty officer's course at Arbroath, not far from Dundee. This lasted for six months and involved more machine-shop work – lathing, filing, drilling, but the exam piece was a new one – which threw the Wrens who had been carefully drilled by the instructors in the standard tests. None of the Wrens could understand the initial drawing and the instructors had to redraw the test design to something they could work from. Even so, Janet didn't do well on this part of the test and, though she passed overall, she wasn't immediately 'rated up' to petty officer.

She was then posted to Anthorne, near Carlisle, working on the base rather than with a squadron, doing big repairs in the workshops. As a leading wren she had not only her own work but was responsible for overseeing other fitters and for signing off their work. Anthorne was a very isolated base, 19 miles from Carlisle itself, but Janet was only there for about six months.

Janet was then made up to acting petty officer and sent back to Lossiemouth, serving there until she completed her service in 1959. She was soon made up to full petty officer and put in charge of publications – keeping the technical manuals updated. Updates would be received and all the manuals were called in and the new sections carefully pasted in – she remembers it was quite hard at times to get the fitters to part with their books and a certain amount of bullying was involved! It wasn't a job she enjoyed as much as her previous ones.

At Lossiemouth she made a particular pal of Molly, who worked in the stores. POs had their own mess which had its own bar, to which guests could be invited. They held Molly's wedding reception there, decorating the whole place with flowers.

Janet took part in a lot of amateur dramatics at her various stations, usually backstage doing costumes or scenery, though she

149

played Mrs Mould, an 'old dragon' in *Madame Louise*, her one and only venture onto the boards. The plays were performed on the air stations but did occasionally go out to local halls and theatres.

Janet's dad always had a motorbike and Janet and her friend Barbara decided to buy an old 500cc Rally between them. They sold that and bought a BSA 250 and when Barbara was posted she sold her share to Janet. Janet then bought a Triumph Tiger Cub which she did many miles on. She didn't have a helmet and wore ordinary clothes (though with extra jumpers).

Asked about her relationship with the pilots, who were all officers in her period of service, she told me,

> We always called out pilots Sir, unless we were on social terms, and off duty. I was never on social terms with an officer. I thought it was social climbing, and was brought up in a family who disapproved of that sort of thing!! My mother was a little disappointed that I didn't go in for a Commission, but I enjoyed my job. I didn't think the junior officers had as much fun as I did anyway.

Janet left the WRNS after marrying Geoff Morley, who worked on radio – they met over an aircraft – and as he was only a leading hand she outranked him! By special dispensation he was allowed into the POs' mess. She taught him to ride her motorbike (he could already drive a car and had once collided with the Minister of Defence's Rolls-Royce). She married Geoff while still serving on 27 December 1958, a civilian wedding rather than a service one. They rented a private house near Elgin where she entertained many of her colleagues. Eventually, Geoff was posted to Yeovilton and the rules said that if your husband was posted you had to follow him, but only when a post became vacant. With no PO's post at Yeovil immediately open, Janet resigned from the service, though as she readily admits she had no idea what she was going to do. She ended up working as a demonstrator in a shop – but she became pregnant shortly after this.

She still admits that she resented having to leave the WRNS – life seemed so much less fun and there were far too many things in civilian life to worry about. She remains a member of the WRNS Association.

Researching Janet Pegden

Finding official material on the FAA stations Janet was posted to has been something of a problem. Very little seems to have survived, or at least been released. Given her rank, and the fact her service was all in peacetime, it would be unlikely that anything mentioning her by name would have been kept anyway, but even so there really isn't much.

The only file from the period I could find on the WRNS Training Establishment at Burghfield was ADM 1/24846, which contains a mass of (partly tongue-in-cheek) correspondence about whether it could be given a ship's name as women were not supposed to be aboard even a nominal ship after dusk. The correspondence runs from 1946 to 1953, when Burghfield was finally named HMS *Dauntless*.

There are a whole series of ships logs for HMS *Fulmar*, the ship's name for RNAS Lossiemouth, in 1958 from ADM 53/149179 onwards, but they say nothing about the work of the station itself, tending just to confirm that the 'watches' were carried out correctly and making occasional mention of ratings (unnamed) being transferred to other stations. There are no extant logs for Yeovilton (HMS *Heron*), Anthorne (HMS *Nuthatch*), Eglinton (HMS *Gannet*) or Burghfield.

Some squadron records for the FAA up to 1955 are at TNA in ADM 207 series. In addition to standard operational reports, ADM 335 series also includes accounts of aircraft trials, a few squadron histories and accident summaries from 1967 onwards. The Fleet Air Arm Museum at Yeovilton holds many squadron record books from the 1950s, as well as the squadron 'line books', which are particularly amusing. Running in parallel with the SRBs, these are a much less formal view of the squadron's activities. Concentrating mainly on the aircrew, they consist of informal (sometimes extremely informal!) photographs, newspaper cuttings, cartoons and poems. For most of them you get the feeling that you need to have been there to understand the exact nature of the joke, but they do give a feel for the life of a FAA crew member at work and at play. Most of the line books cover peacetime operations but there are one or two from the Second World War and others from Korea and other wars. Yeovilton also has some material on Wrens in the FAA.

FAA accident reports for the 1950s are usually in ADM 1 series at

TNA in Kew. Searching on the key word 'Accident' for the year 1954 and restricting the series to ADM 1 actually brings up seventy-nine results – many actually refer to accidents that occurred in 1953, but where enquiries continued to 1954. One report leaps out as a likely one, however, in ADM 1/25323: 'Aircraft Accidents: Firefly TB MB 566 on 8.3.54 at RNAS Eglinton. Includes 1 photograph depicting: Firefly T Mk 2: damage to mainplane Rib 11. Dated 1954'. This is, indeed, the report on the accident Janet witnessed and I've quoted her section verbatim because it matched so accurately the story she told me.

INDEX

153